VACATION BIBLE SCHOOL IDEAS AND SUMMERTIME FUN

GOD'S GIFTS OF SUMMER

by
Susan Schneck
and
Mary Strohl

illustrated by
Susan Schneck

Cover by Kathryn Hyndman

Shining Star Publications, Copyright © 1989
A division of Good Apple, Inc.

ISBN No. 0-86653-477-6

Standardized Subject Code TA ac

Printing No. 9876

Shining Star Publications
A Division of Good Apple, Inc.
Box 299
Carthage, IL 62321-0299

The purchase of this book entitles the buyer to reproduce student activity pages for classroom use only. Any other use requires written permission from Shining Star Publications.

All rights reserved. Printed in the United States of America.

Unless otherwise indicated, the King James Version of the Bible was used in preparing the activities in this book.

DEDICATION

To Jenny and Katie,
my most precious gifts from God

Love,
Mother

To Natalie and Sarah:
May you always grow in God's grace

Love,
Aunt Mary

TABLE OF CONTENTS

A Word to Parents and Teachers 4

Memory Verses
- Loving Links 5
- Lift Up Thy Spirit! 8
- God's Treasure Chest 10
- Sunburst Scriptures 12
- Christian Service Cards 13
- Slide into Summer Bible Verses 14
- Time to Pray 16
- Verse String Along 17
- Summertime Flowers 18
- God's Gift of the Spirit Puzzle 20
- Lacing Cards to Share with Others 22
- Love God Maze 25
- The Living Light 26
- Books of the Old Testament 27
- Books of the New Testament 28

Summertime Crafts
- Pool or Tub Toys 29
- Summertime Tattoos 31
- Weave the Colors of Summer 32
- Sun Visor Scriptures 33
- Scrimshaw Pictures 35
- Dove Mobile 36
- Wind Socks 37
- God's Helper Litter Bags 39
- Growing Love Posies 40
- Sun Camera "Photos" 42
- Hopping Bunnies Race 43
- Leaping Frogs 44
- Sun Catchers 45
- Fun Time Rock-a-longs 46
- Weekly Prayer Folder 48
- Bubbles Up and Away! 50
- Heart Sun Sparklers 51
- Pop-Up Greetings 52
- "Sandy" Paint 54
- Sunshiny Paint 55

Games
- Bible School Chant 56
- Red Rover Old Testament Game 57
- Moses at the Red Sea Beanbag Toss 58
- Daniel in the Lion's Den 60
- Wall of Jericho 61
- Leap Frog 62
- Jordan River Regatta 62
- Noah's Ark Charades 62

Camel Tag	64
Outdoor Board Game	65
Jump over Jordan Game	67
Vacation Bible School Field Day	68
Obstacle Courses	69
Over the Mountains and Under the Sky Relay	70
Manna Race	71
Pharaoh's Goblet Race	72
Deliver Grain to Joseph's Granary	73

Snacks
Frigid Frosties	74
Watermelon Fizz	74
Blueberry Bubbles	75
Fruity Sun Tea	75
Loaves and Fishes Snack	76
Bumps on a Log	76
Peanut Butter Clay	76
Sunburst Sandwiches	76

Songs
Summertime Fun Finger Play	77
I Can Listen to My Jesus	78
God's Garden	79
Joy Song and Finger Play	79
Buddy Song and Dance	80

Puppets
Bible Story Players and Theater	81
Bible Story Theater	82
Bible Story Players	83
Puppets in a Cup	86
God's Favorite Poem	90
Cloth and Cardboard Roll Puppet	93
Daisy Poem and Puppet	95

A WORD TO PARENTS & TEACHERS

God's gifts make summer special. New life is budding and blossoming all around us. The miracles of sunshine and cooling rain abound. It is a time to enjoy friendships and favorite outdoor activities. We should all be more aware of and thankful for these gifts.

Vacation Bible School is a unique time to capture children's interest. They are relaxed and refreshed—away from all the school year routines. The memory verses, crafts, games, songs, puppets and snacks are planned to enhance your teaching curriculum. Try to make each lesson you teach an enjoyable, concrete experience children can take home to share with family and friends.

We hope our suggestions will instill a joy and appreciation for God's gifts this summer.

God's blessings with each of you,

Mary and Sue

MEMORY VERSES
LOVING LINKS

Your children can learn Bible verses more easily if you give them something to manipulate as they work with a verse. Reproduce one pattern for each word of the verse on heavy tagboard. Print words to your verse on each piece. Use the loving links pattern together as a class or individually. Hang them in the classroom or allow the children to take them home as a reminder of your lesson. There are four patterns for a variety of verses.

MATERIALS:

Loving links pattern
Heavy tagboard
Scissors
Crayons or markers

BOY PATTERN

POSSIBLE VERSE:

Serve the Lord with gladness: come before his presence with singing. Psalm 100:2

GIRL PATTERN

DIRECTIONS:
1. Color the links and cut them out.
2. Link them as shown and read the verse together.

DAISY PATTERN

LAMB PATTERN

POSSIBLE VERSE:
And be ye kind one to another, tenderhearted, forgiving one another, even as God for Christ's sake hath forgiven you.
Ephesians 4:32

LIFT UP THY SPIRIT!

Sharing the good news with others can be an uplifting experience for your class this summer! Use this balloon pattern to help children learn short Bible verses by decorating balloons and hanging them in church halls or from trees outside for inspiration. You may want to have a helium balloon launch to spread the word to your community. Ask children to write their names and the church phone number on the backs of the balloons. Launch them into the sky together after a short devotional. Hopefully, you'll get calls from those who find the balloons.

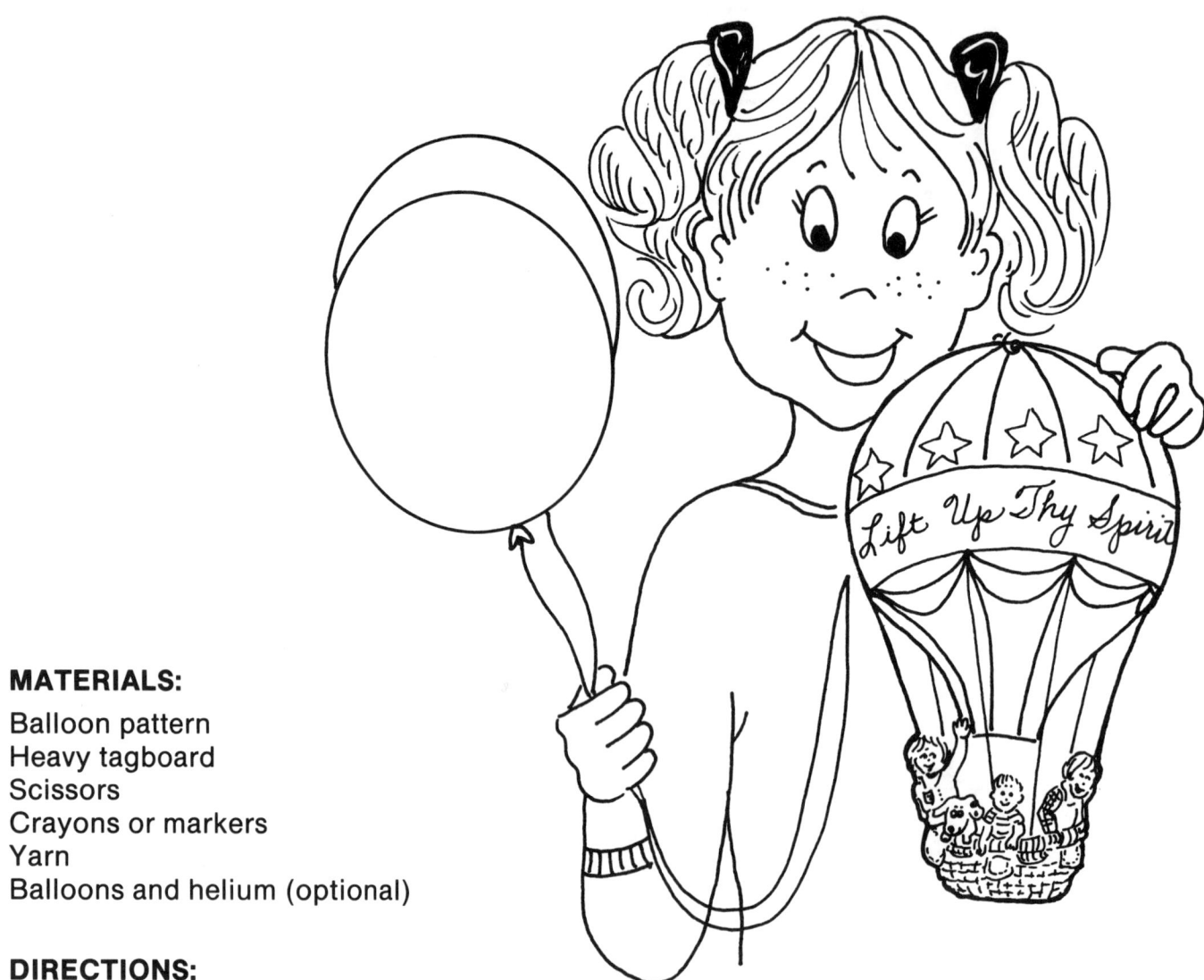

MATERIALS:

Balloon pattern
Heavy tagboard
Scissors
Crayons or markers
Yarn
Balloons and helium (optional)

DIRECTIONS:

1. Print special Bible verses in the large areas at the center of the balloons.
2. On heavy tagboard, reproduce enough balloons for each child.
3. Color and cut out the balloons.
4. Punch a hole and hang with yarn or string.
5. Use as hallway decorations or reproduce on light paper and attach to several helium balloons to send God's loving message to others.

POSSIBLE VERSE:

. . . I bare you on eagles' wings, and brought you unto myself.   Exodus 19:4

BALLOON PATTERN

GOD'S TREASURE CHEST

Fill a paper or plastic egg carton with paper gems for your class to use with memory verses. You can make several sets of gems for different verses. Put the gem sets in envelopes. When a child has a spare moment, he or she can choose an envelope and put the gems into the treasure chest to read the verse.

MATERIALS:

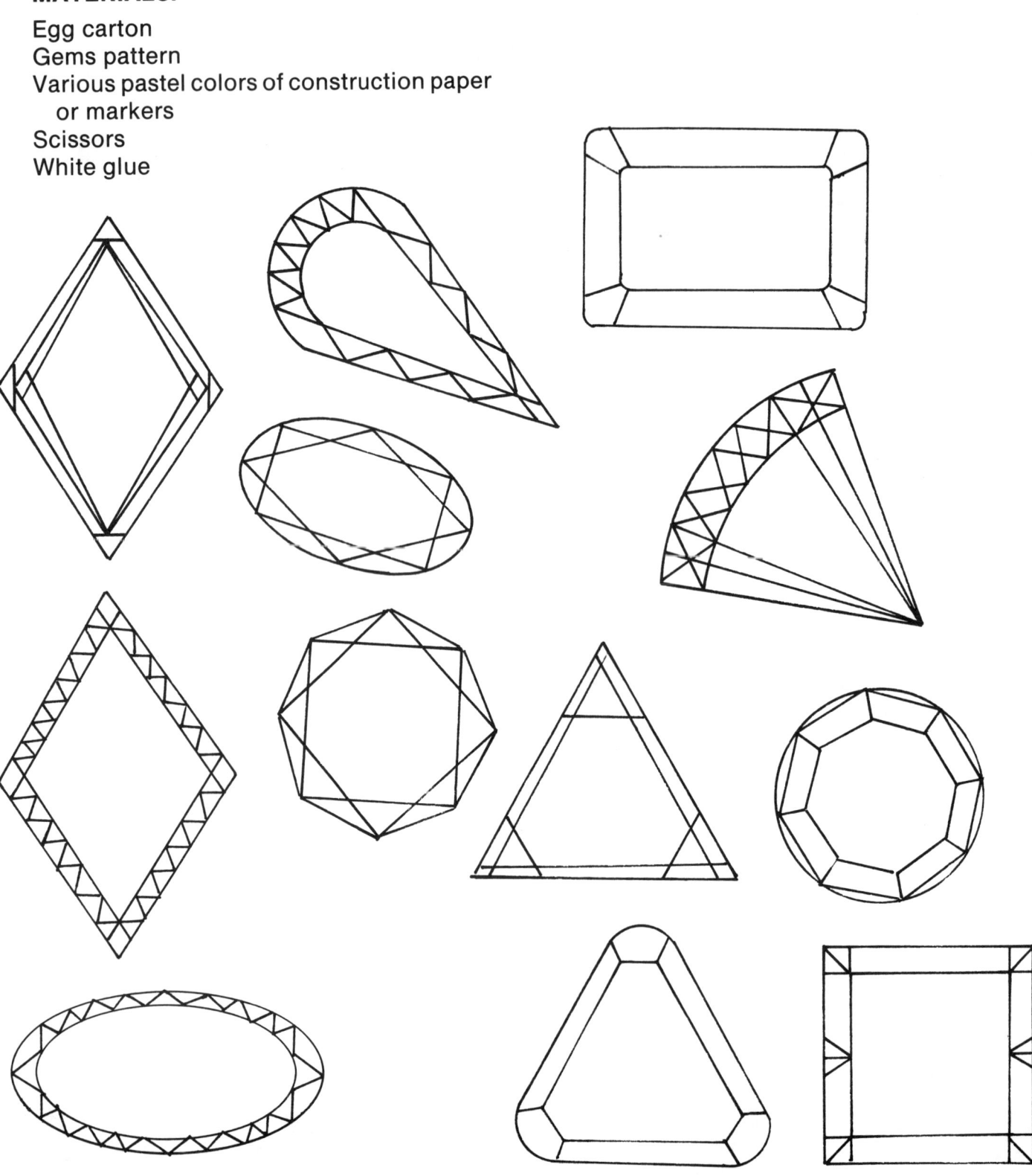

Egg carton
Gems pattern
Various pastel colors of construction paper
   or markers
Scissors
White glue

DIRECTIONS:

1. Decorate egg carton using the label provided or with buttons and yarn. Glue to carton.
2. Trace or copy the gems on construction or heavy white paper. Color with markers if you like.
3. Write a word or phrase of a Bible verse on each gem. Number the back of each gem in the correct order so children can self-check their progress.
4. Ask the children to put the gems in the treasure chest in the proper order to read the verse.

POSSIBLE VERSES:

Ye are my friends, if ye do whatsoever I command you. John 15:14

For God so loved the world, that he gave his only begotten Son . . . . John 3:16

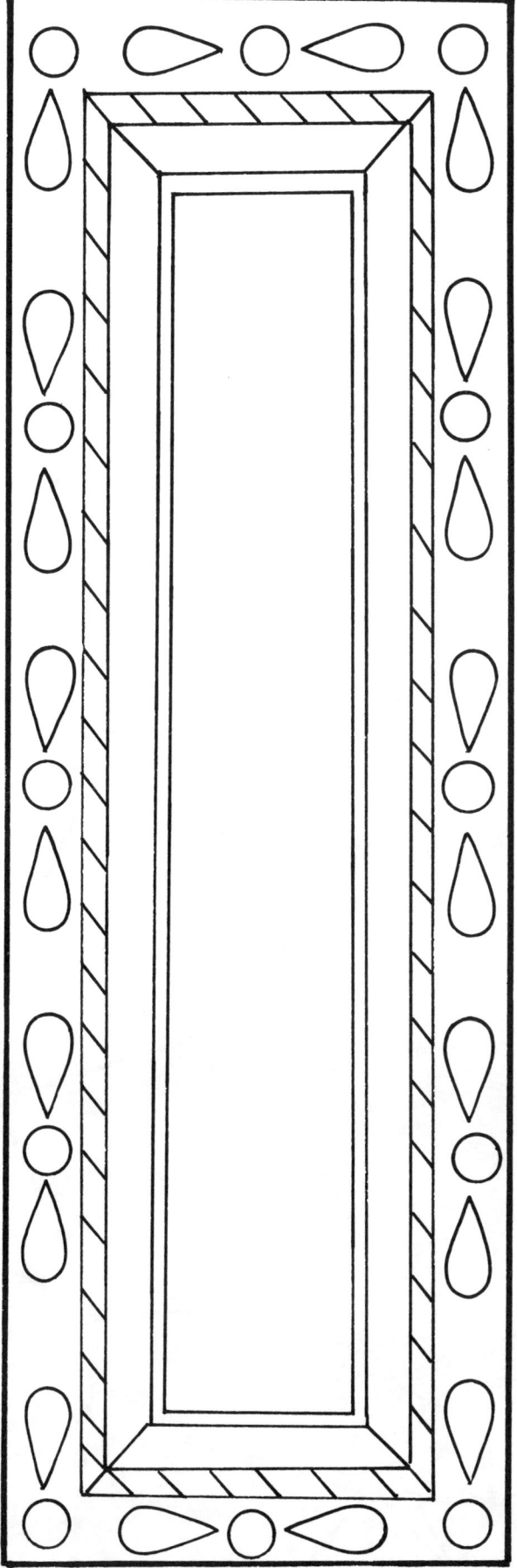

SUNBURST SCRIPTURES

This is another manipulative that will help children remember verses. After they have decorated them, they'll take pride in showing them to their friends and family.

MATERIALS:

Sunburst pattern, yellow construction paper, red and/or orange tissue paper, white glue diluted in one third as much water, scissors

DIRECTIONS:

1. Write the desired verse or devotional on the inner triangles as shown, starting with the triangle with the arrow.
2. Reproduce one sun for each child on yellow construction paper.
3. Children cut out their suns.
4. Fold the sun rays to the center and decorate the backs of the triangles with tissue, using the diluted glue. It doesn't matter if the tissue is neatly pasted. The effects of layers are quite appealing.
5. Children open the sun rays to read the verse.

Shining Star Publications, Copyright © 1989, A division of Good Apple, Inc.

SS1813

CHRISTIAN SERVICE CARDS

Children can learn to help at home or at church by pledging to do services on these cards. Reproduce on pastel paper. Each child can fill in services he/she will perform at home or church.

MATERIALS:

Card reproducibles
Pencils or crayons

DIRECTIONS:

1. Cut the cards apart.
2. Fill in the cards with services you will do at home or church.
3. Give the cards to the person you will be helping. God loves those that help others!

VERSES FOR BACKS OF CARDS:

A friend loveth at all times . . . . Proverbs 17:17	And whatsoever ye do in word or deed, do all in the name of the Lord Jesus . . . . Colossians 3:17
. . . ever follow that which is good, both among yourselves, and to all men. I Thessalonians 5:15	Blessed are the peacemakers: for they shall be called the children of God. Matthew 5:9

SLIDE INTO SUMMER BIBLE VERSES

Children will be reminded of God's gifts of fun in this memory verse activity. They can use their sliders to master new verses and to review the old ones. Encourage them to read the verses a little more smoothly each time. Whee! You're all sliding into summer Vacation Bible School!

MATERIALS:

Slide reproducible
Slider reproducible
Stapler

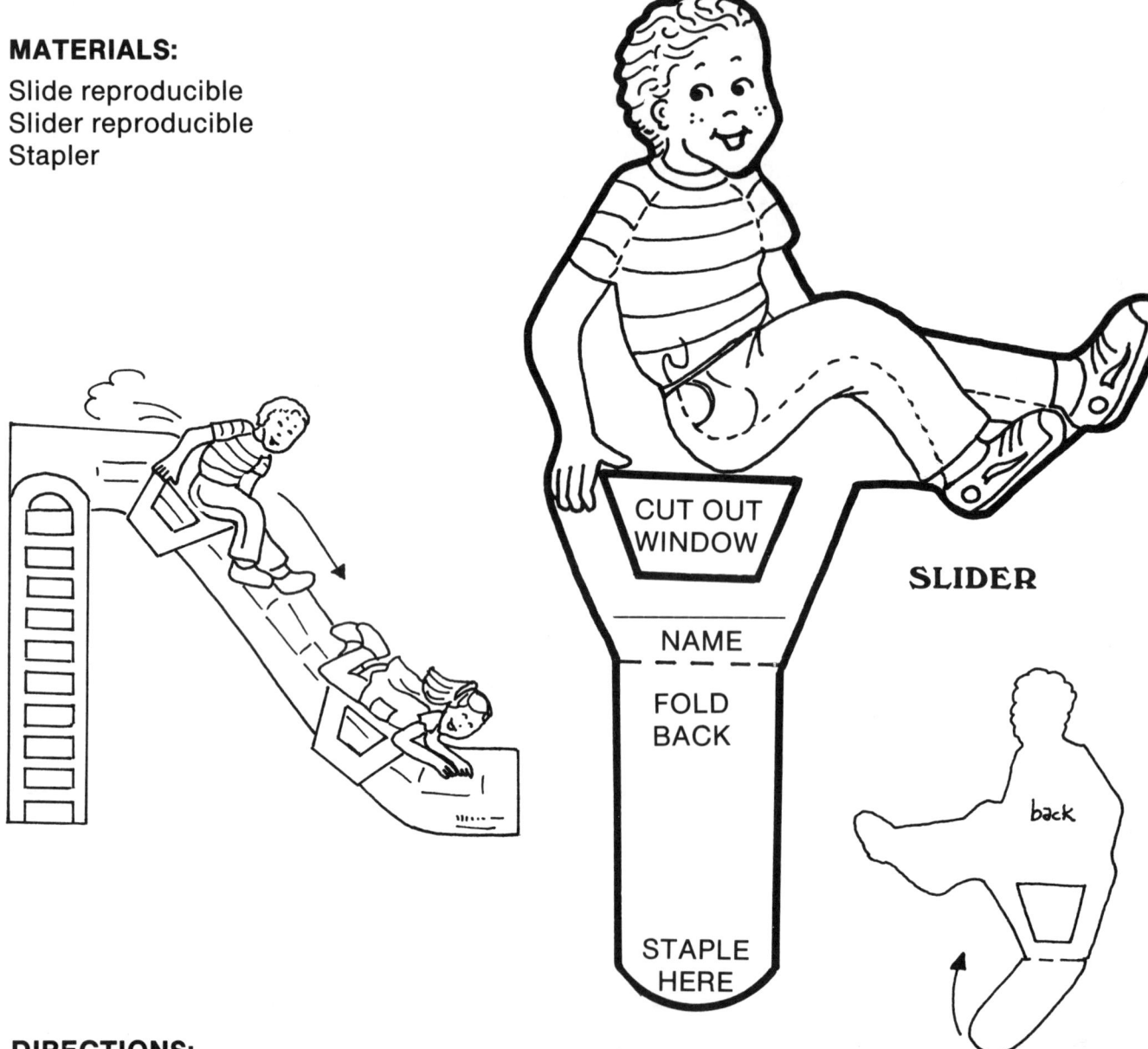

DIRECTIONS:

1. Reproduce enough "sliders" for each of your students to personalize, color, cut out and assemble. Note: You will need to help them cut out the word windows.
2. Make a copy of the slide reproducible. (Keep master pattern for later needs.) Print your verse clearly on the slides in the space provided. Reproduce as many as you need on tagboard. Laminate the strips before you cut them out for long-lasting fun!
3. Children slip their "sliders" down the slide, reading the verse as they go.

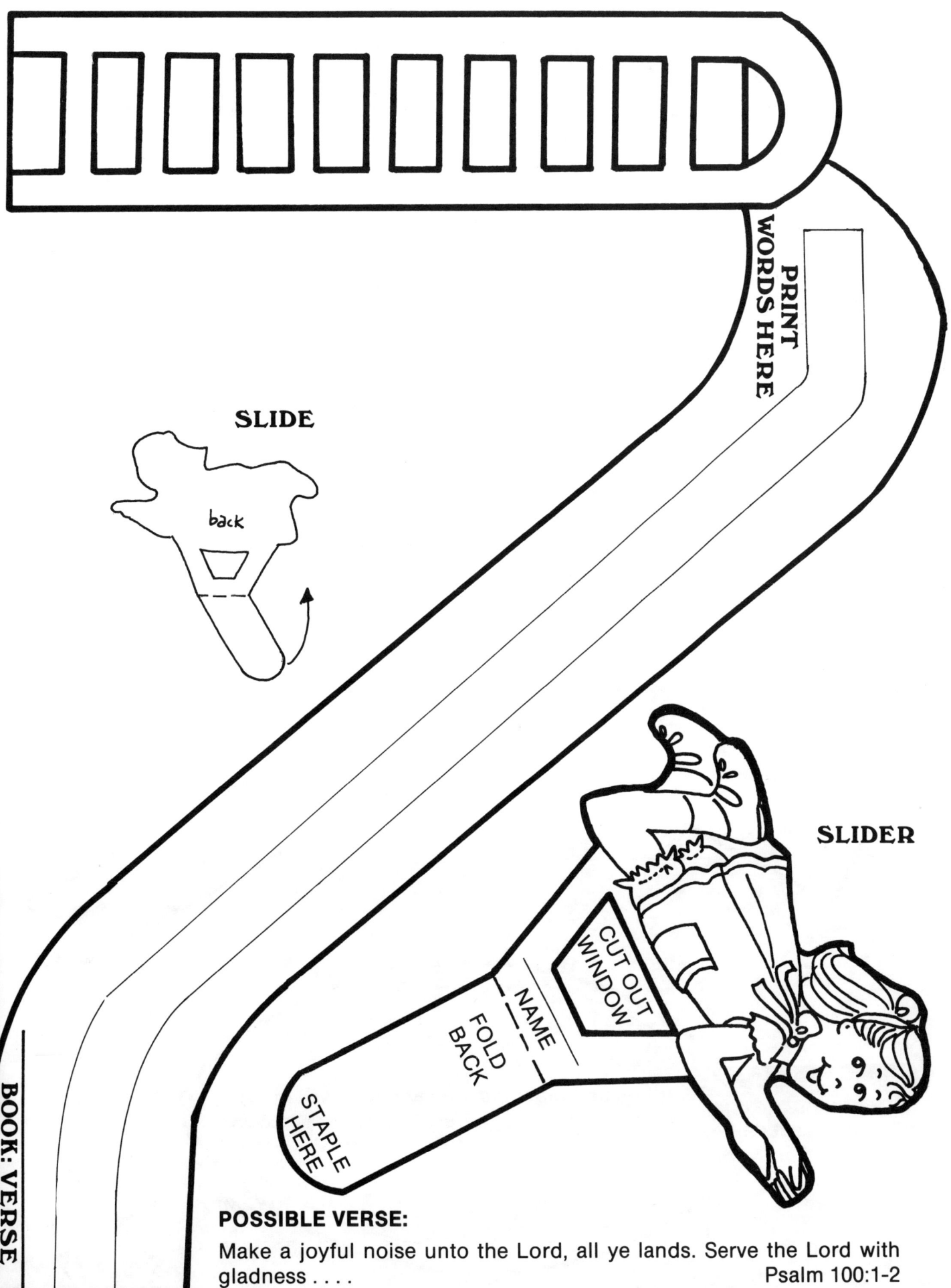

POSSIBLE VERSE:

Make a joyful noise unto the Lord, all ye lands. Serve the Lord with gladness . . . .
Psalm 100:1-2

TIME TO PRAY

Children can practice telling time with the clocks after they have learned the verse. Use small, pastel paper plates or plain ones. Copy the verse and clock hands on plain paper for each child.

12
1
2
3
4
5
6
7
8
9
10
11

MATERIALS:

Verse cutout
Clock hands cutout
Paper plate
Glue
Brass brad
Scissors
Crayons

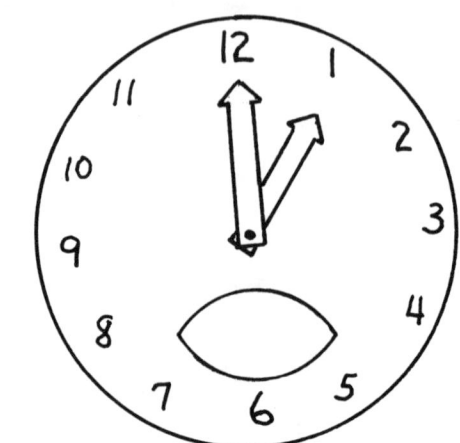

DIRECTIONS:

1. Cut out verse and clock hands.
2. Glue verse to paper plate as shown.
3. Put hands on plate and insert brad at dot. Bend brad back.
4. Add numbers and decorate.

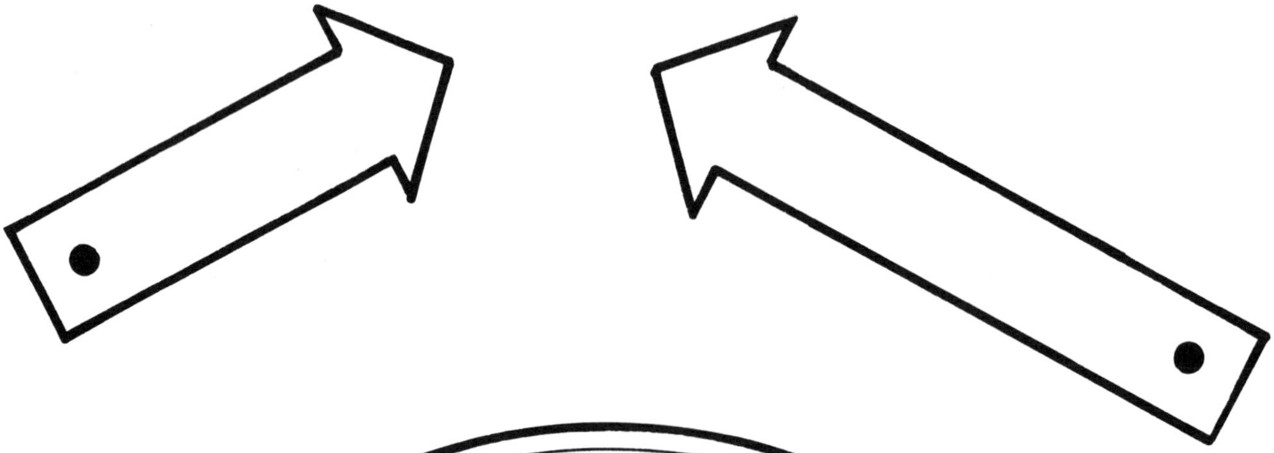

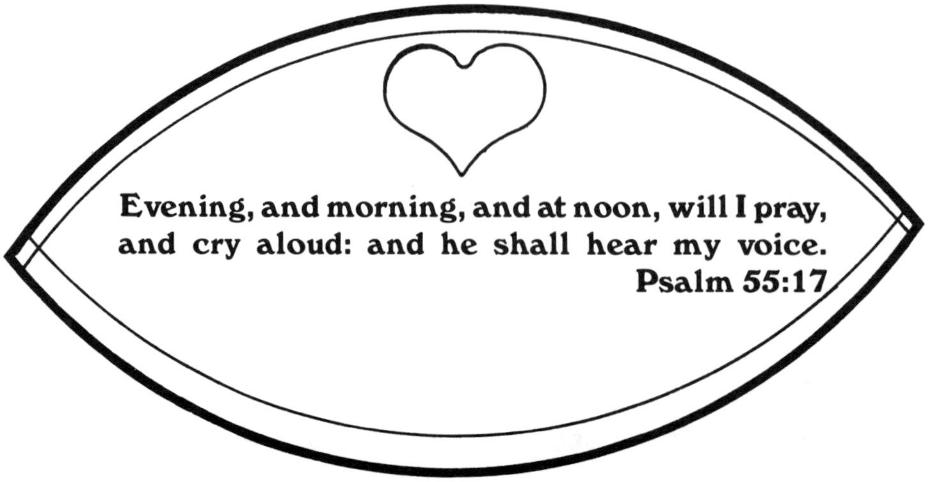
Evening, and morning, and at noon, will I pray, and cry aloud: and he shall hear my voice.
Psalm 55:17

VERSE STRING ALONG

Write verse words or phrases on small, pastel-colored cards. You can use a different color for each verse. Keep the verses in envelopes for children to use during spare time. Attach firmly to a large flannel board in random order. Add a thumbtack beside each word. At the top of the board hang a long string or yarn.

MATERIALS:
Verse word cards
Thumbtacks
Yarn or string

DIRECTIONS:
Use the string to connect the words to the Bible verse in proper order.

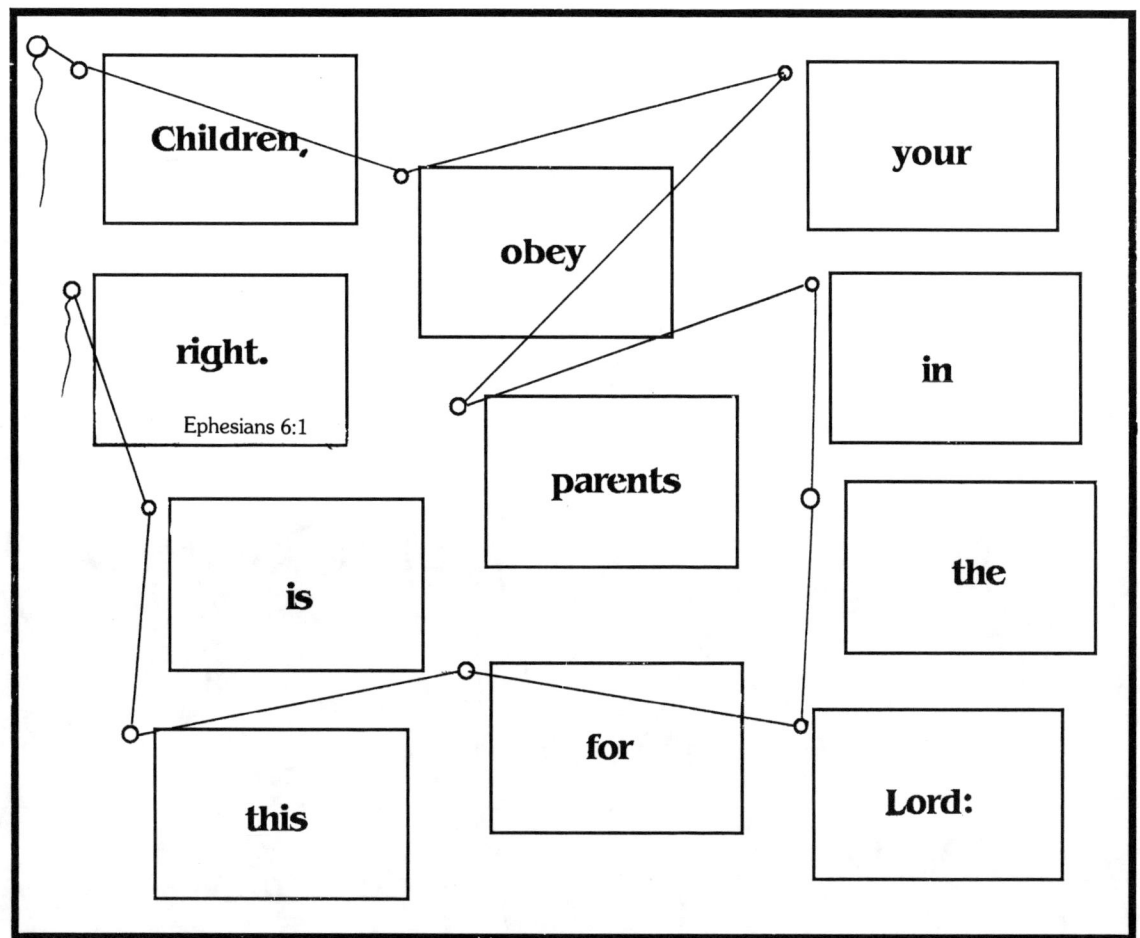

SAMPLE VERSE:

Children, obey your parents in the Lord: for this is right.   Ephesians 6:1

SUMMERTIME FLOWERS

Enjoy God's gift of beautiful summer flowers with this puzzle. Select a verse and write the words on the flowers. Be sure to write on the correct flower for the child to finish in the proper order. Reproduce flowers and flower outline puzzle for each child.

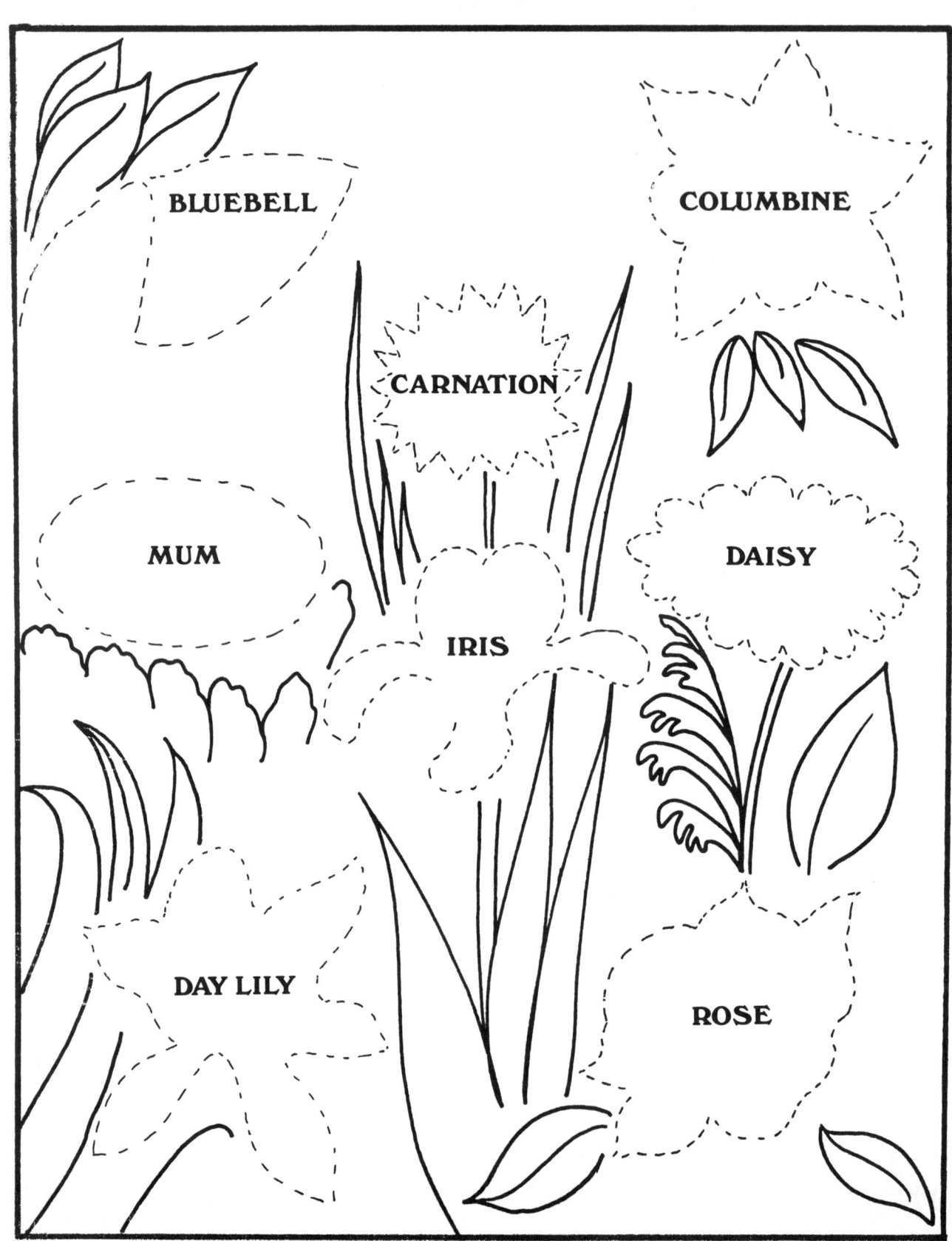

DIRECTIONS:
1. Color the flowers and the puzzle background.
2. Cut out the flowers.
3. Glue them to the background.
4. Read the verse that you've made.

VERSE:

The grass withereth, the flower fadeth: but the word of our God shall stand for ever.   Isaiah 40:8

Shining Star Publications, Copyright © 1989, A division of Good Apple, Inc.   19   SS1813

GOD'S GIFT OF THE SPIRIT PUZZLE

Use this puzzle featuring fruits in the same manner as the Summertime Flowers on the preceding pages.

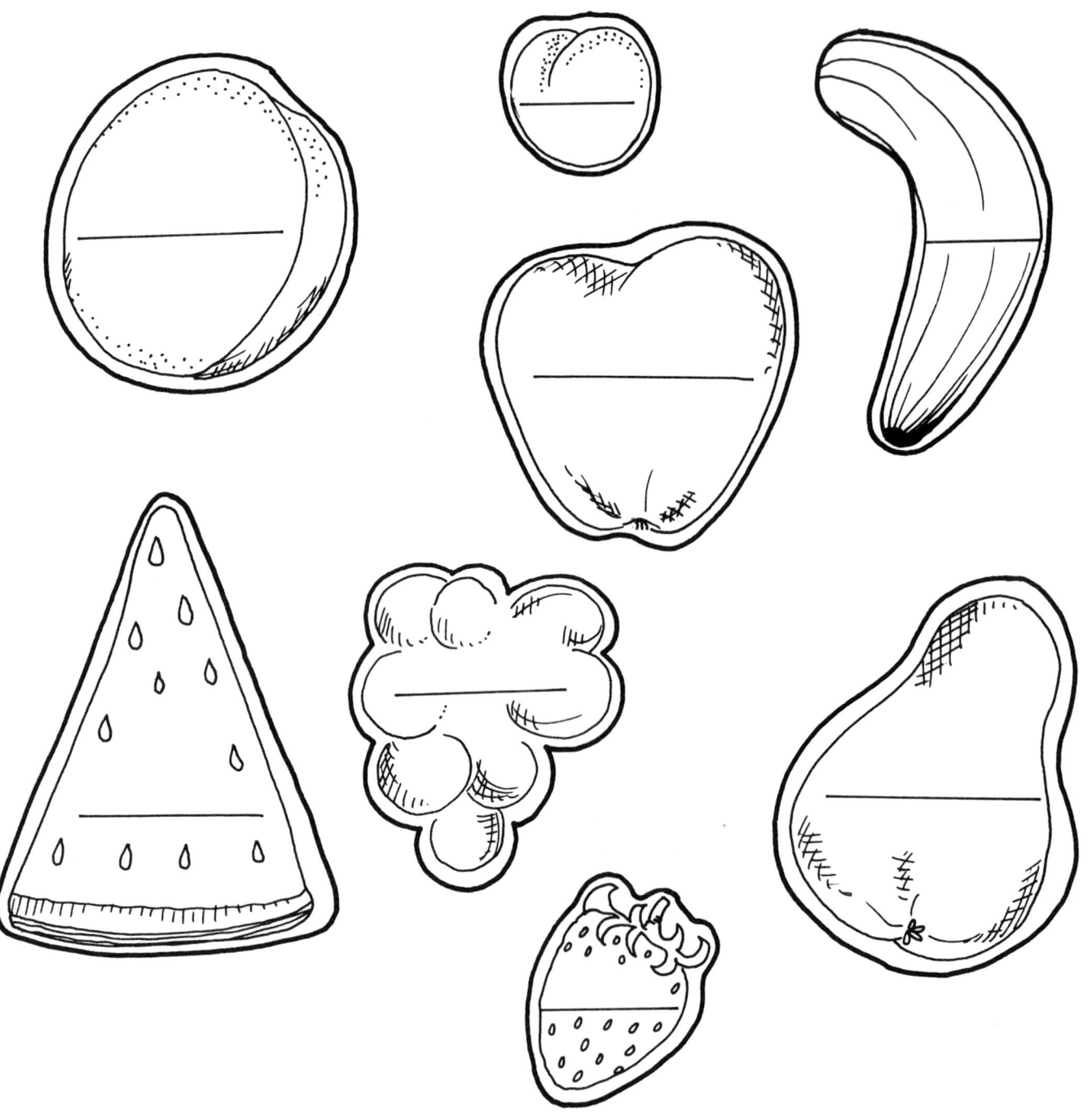

VERSE:
And now abideth faith, hope, charity, these three; but the greatest of these is charity.
I Corinthians 13:13

FRUIT BOWL PUZZLE

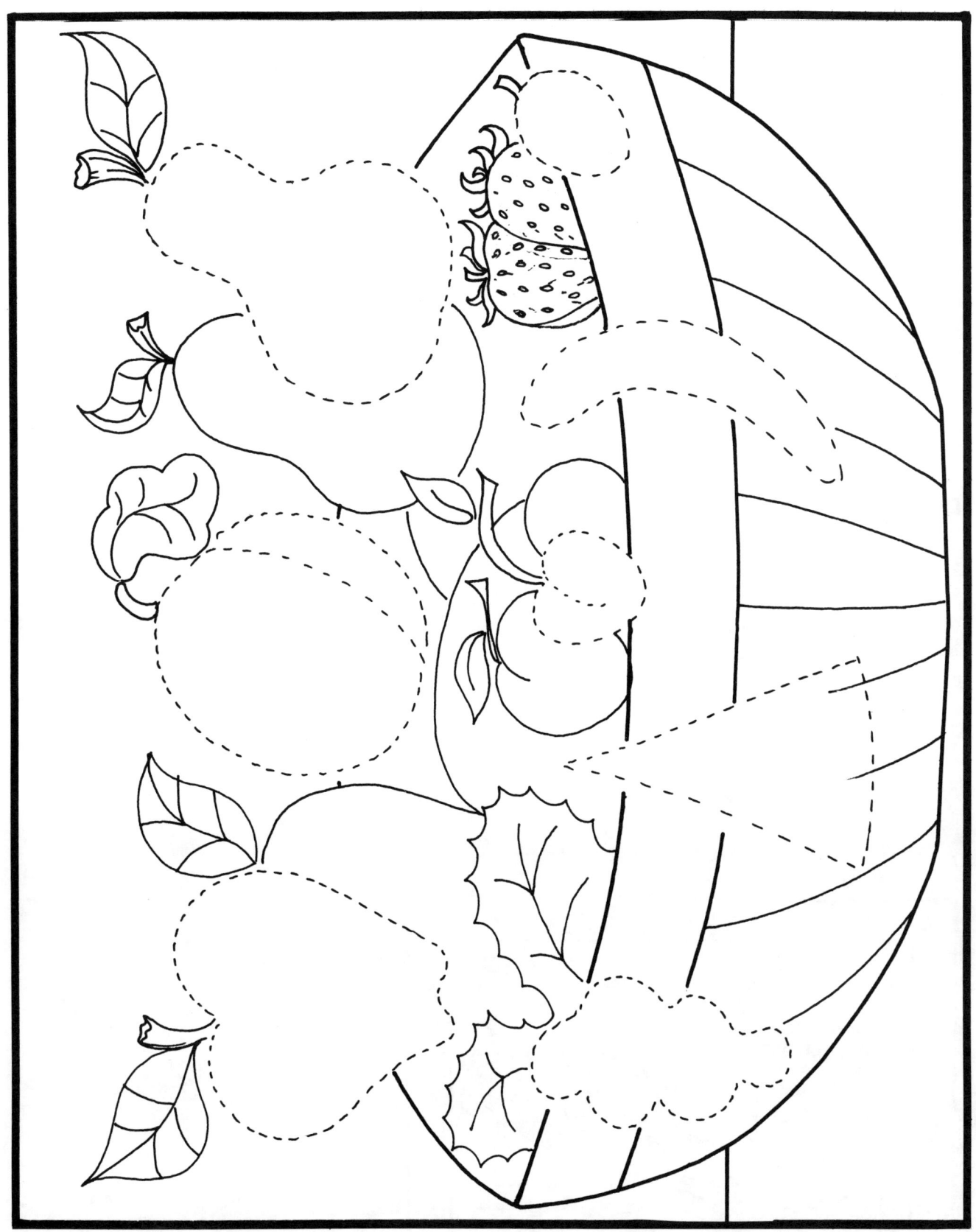

LACING CARDS TO SHARE WITH OTHERS

Reproduce a card and a quotation on heavy tagboard for each child to color and lace with yarn. Use big darning needles that are not as sharp as regular needles. They should be used only under supervision. Ask the children to give the cards to special loved ones.

MATERIALS:

Lacing-card picture and quotation
Crayons or markers
1 sheet construction paper
Fine yarn
Darning needle
Scissors
Glue

DIRECTIONS:

1. Cut the greeting and card apart in the center.
2. Color the picture.
3. Use darning needle and yarn to stitch the cards.
4. Fold construction paper in half.
5. Glue stitched card to outside.
6. Glue quote card inside.

Verily, verily, I say unto you, He that believeth on me hath everlasting life. I am that bread of life.   John 6:47, 48

This card was lovingly laced by

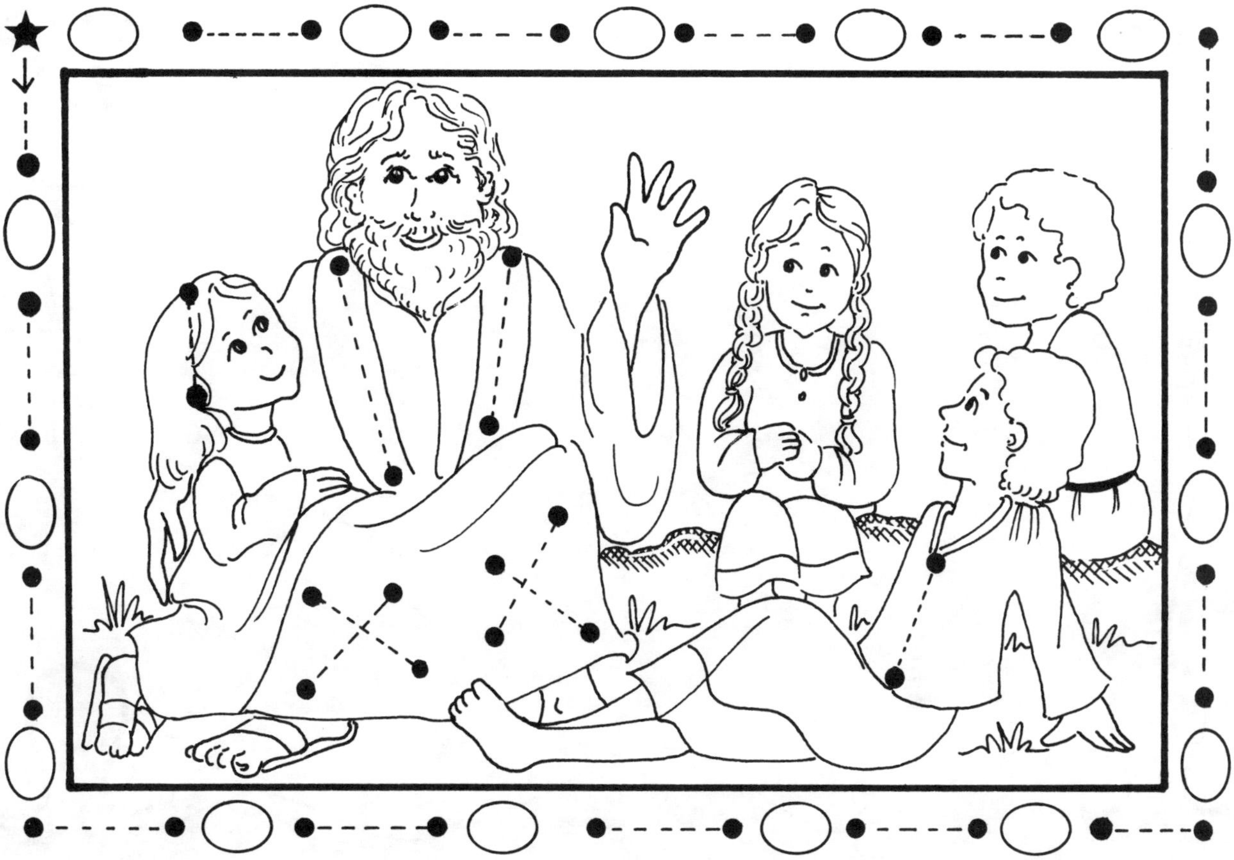

_____

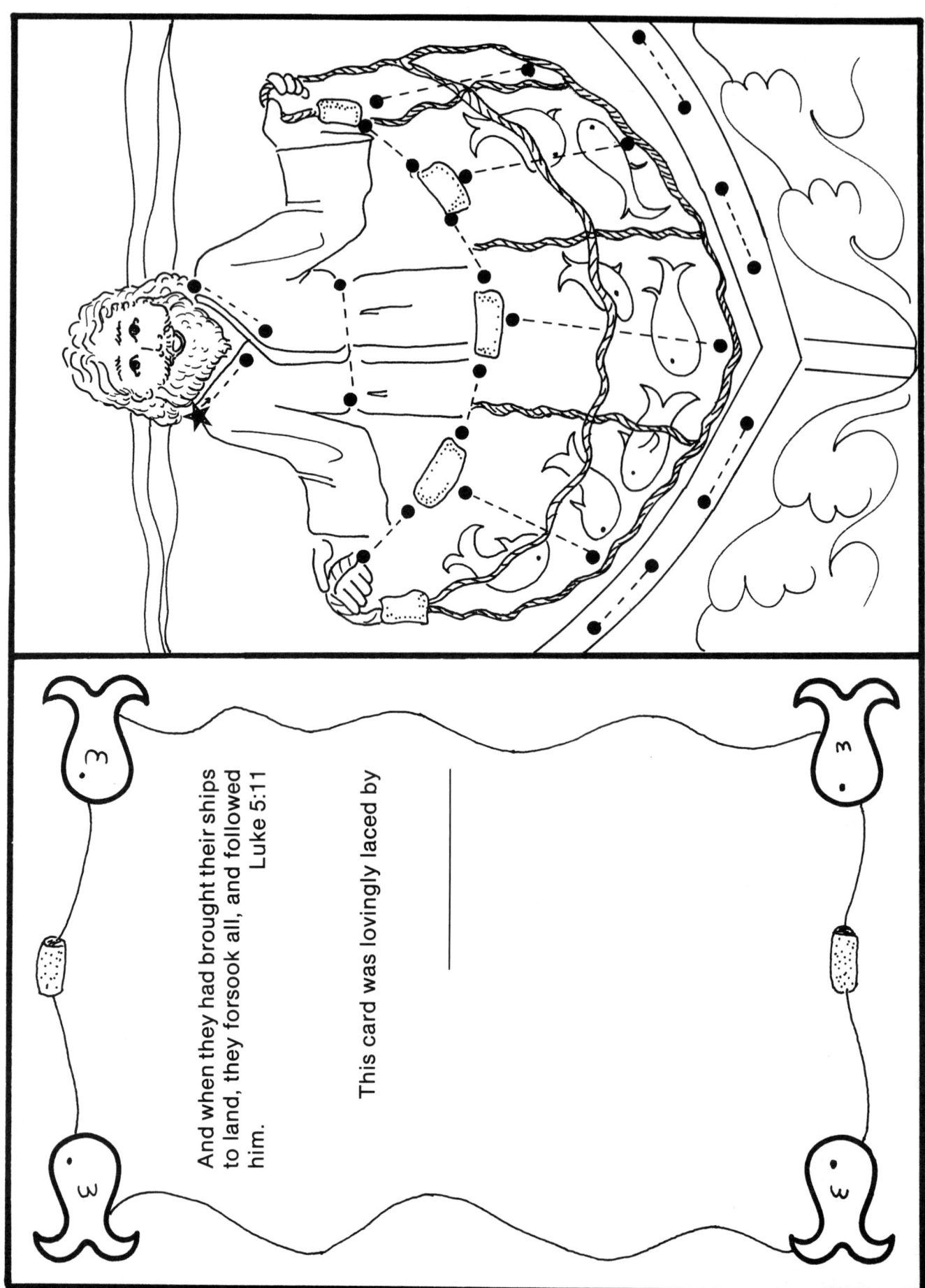

And when they had brought their ships to land, they forsook all, and followed him.
Luke 5:11

This card was lovingly laced by _____

LOVE GOD MAZE

As children move their pencils through this maze, they will find a special message. Copy one maze for each child.

THE LIVING LIGHT

Follow the dots to complete the picture. Reproduce one for each child.

Thy word is a lamp unto my feet,
and a light unto my path.
Psalm 119:105

BOOKS OF THE OLD TESTAMENT

The first seventeen books of the Old Testament are in the puzzle below. Can you find them all? Look across, down and diagonally. This is a big challenge.

- Genesis
- Exodus
- Leviticus
- Numbers
- Deuteronomy
- Joshua
- Judges
- Ruth
- Samuel (1 & 2)
- Kings (1 & 2)
- Chronicles (1 & 2)
- Ezra
- Nehemiah
- Esther

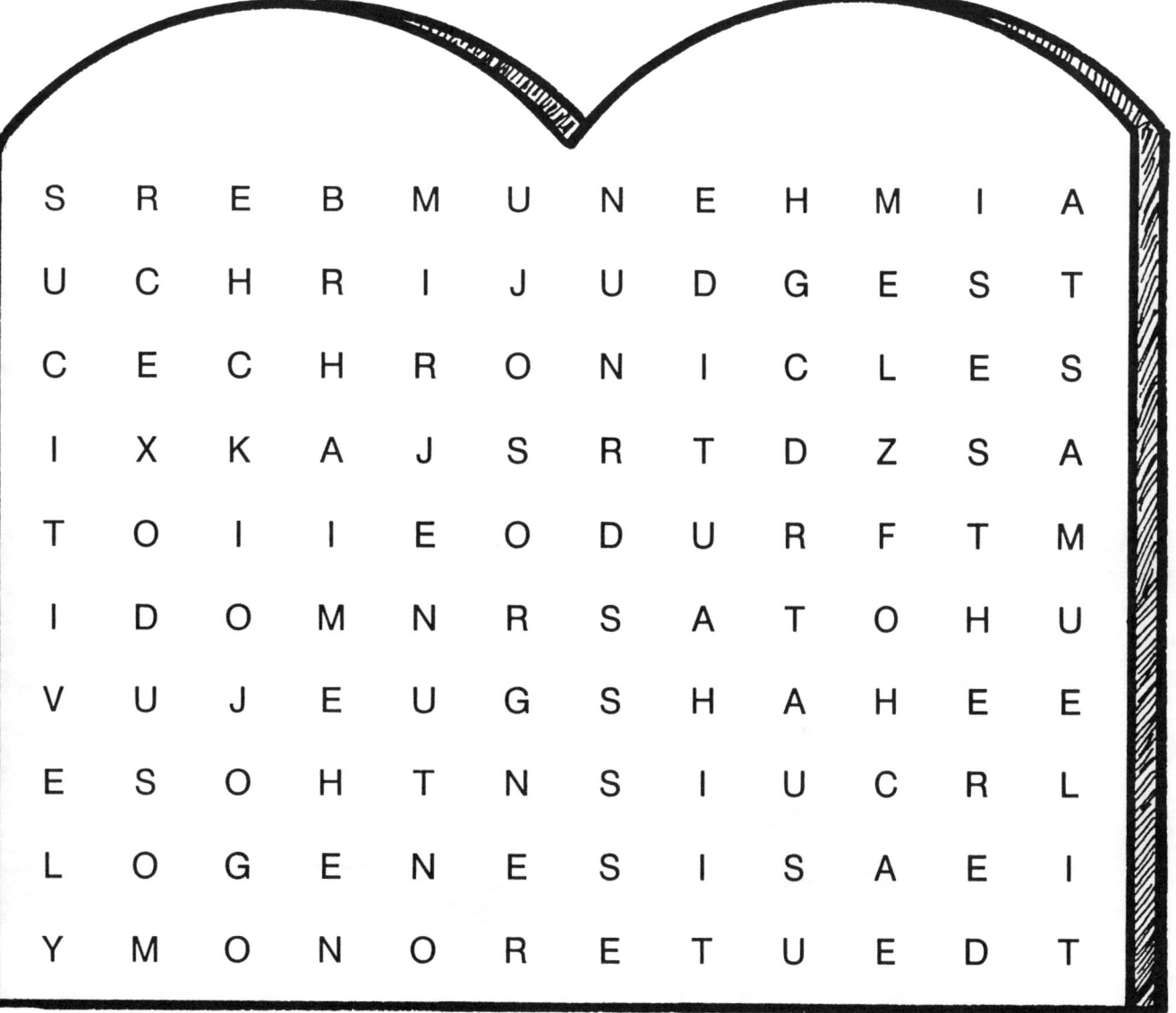

BOOKS OF THE NEW TESTAMENT

The first twelve books of the New Testament are in the puzzle below. Look for them across, down and diagonally. Copy one puzzle for each child. This is another big challenge.

Matthew
Mark
Luke
John
Acts
Romans

Corinthians (1 & 2)
Galatians
Ephesians
Philippians
Colossians

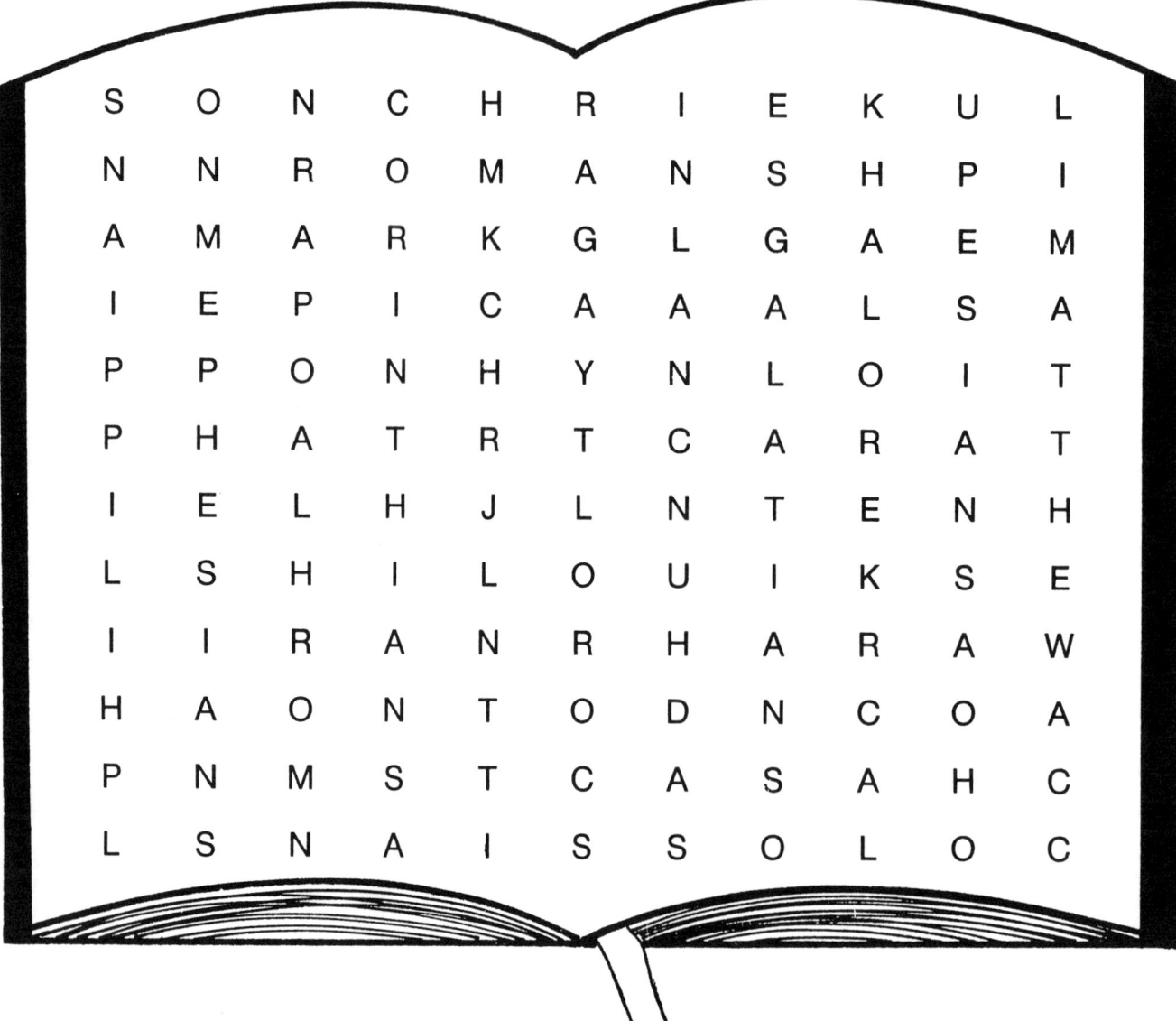

SUMMERTIME CRAFTS
POOL OR TUB TOYS

God provides us with cool water to enjoy in the summer. Children will enjoy making these pool and tub toys that really float. If you have access to a small, inflatable pool, children can enjoy having races by blowing their toys across the pool.

MATERIALS:

Reproduce the patterns on heavy tagboard for tracing.
one 10¼" foam plastic plate per toy
Patterns
Ballpoint pen
Scissors
Crayons

29

Shining Star Publications, Copyright © 1989, A division of Good Apple, Inc.

SS1813

DIRECTIONS:

1. Use a ballpoint pen to trace around patterns on plastic plate. Add details as desired. NOTE: Some children may have an easier time if they cut off the rim of the plate before tracing.
2. Cut out pieces and assemble as shown.
3. Enjoy your new toy in the pool or bathtub.

SUMMERTIME TATTOOS

These wash-off tattoos are great fun for children to play with outside. Be sure to use water-based markers. Simple designs are the best.

MATERIALS:

Tissue paper cut in small squares
Watercolor markers
Sponge
Bowl of water

DIRECTIONS:

1. Color tattoos on tissue paper, using markers. If you want to have words on your tattoo, write the words backwards on the tissue.
2. Wet the area where you want the tattoo. Lay the tissue on that spot (color side down). Place damp sponge over the tissue for a few seconds.
3. Remove sponge and tissue, leaving "tattoo" on skin.

WEAVE THE COLORS OF SUMMER

Enjoy the sunshine outside while children learn to weave a small banner. Sing songs or tell stories during the activity. Cut paper plates ahead of time with a knife as shown in the diagram. Add a short phrase around the outer rim with a crayon.

MATERIALS:

Paper plates, with strips cut, as shown
Narrow ribbon of various colors
Scissors
Tape

DIRECTIONS:

1. Cut ribbons into 5" or 6" lengths.
2. Weave the ribbons onto the paper plate, going over and under the strips. Go under and over for the next ribbon.
3. Continue until the plate is covered with ribbon.
4. Tape ends on the back of the plate.
5. Hang in a special place.

Shining Star Publications, Copyright © 1989, A division of Good Apple, Inc. SS1813

SUN VISOR SCRIPTURES

Use the simple patterns to create colorful summertime visors that show the world a special message, too! Reproduce the pattern on tagboard.

MATERIALS:
Visor patterns
Scissors
Crayons or markers
Yarn (two 15" pieces)
Transparent tape
Tagboard

DIRECTIONS:
1. Cut out the band and visor along the heavy lines.
2. Decorate with crayons or markers.
3. Cut slits carefully.
4. Tape the slit edge behind the straight edge of the band. Bend slightly to ease the curve as you tape.
5. Punch out the holes and attach the yarn to each. Tie on head.

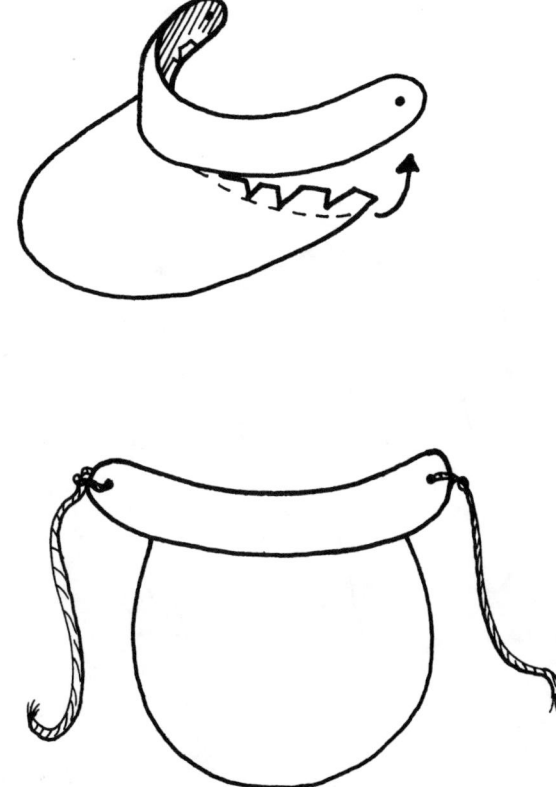

VISOR PATTERNS

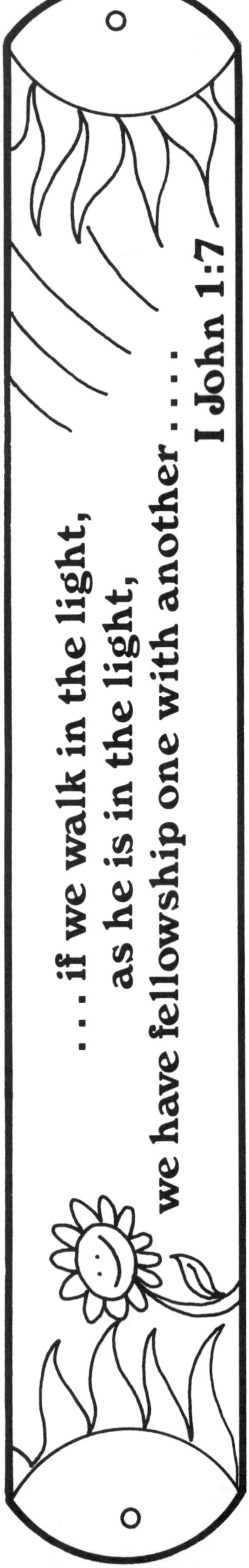

HEADBAND PATTERN

...if we walk in the light, as he is in the light, we have fellowship one with another..... I John 1:7

VISOR PATTERN

SCRIMSHAW PICTURES

Scrimshaw is the art that whalers developed by carving the teeth of whales. Some grocery stores will give you Styrofoam meat trays or you can ask the children to bring them along to Vacation Bible School.

MATERIALS:

Styrofoam meat tray
Pencil
Large sharp nail
Black shoe polish
Paper towels

DIRECTIONS:

1. Draw or trace your design onto the meat tray, using a pencil.
2. Use the nail to etch the picture into the tray.
3. Rub shoe polish into lines with a paper towel. Use a clean towel to wipe off excess.

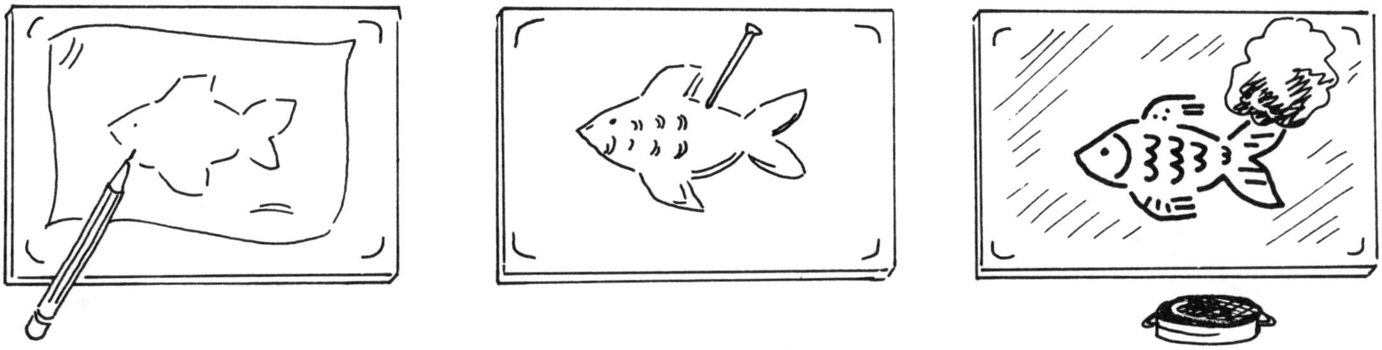

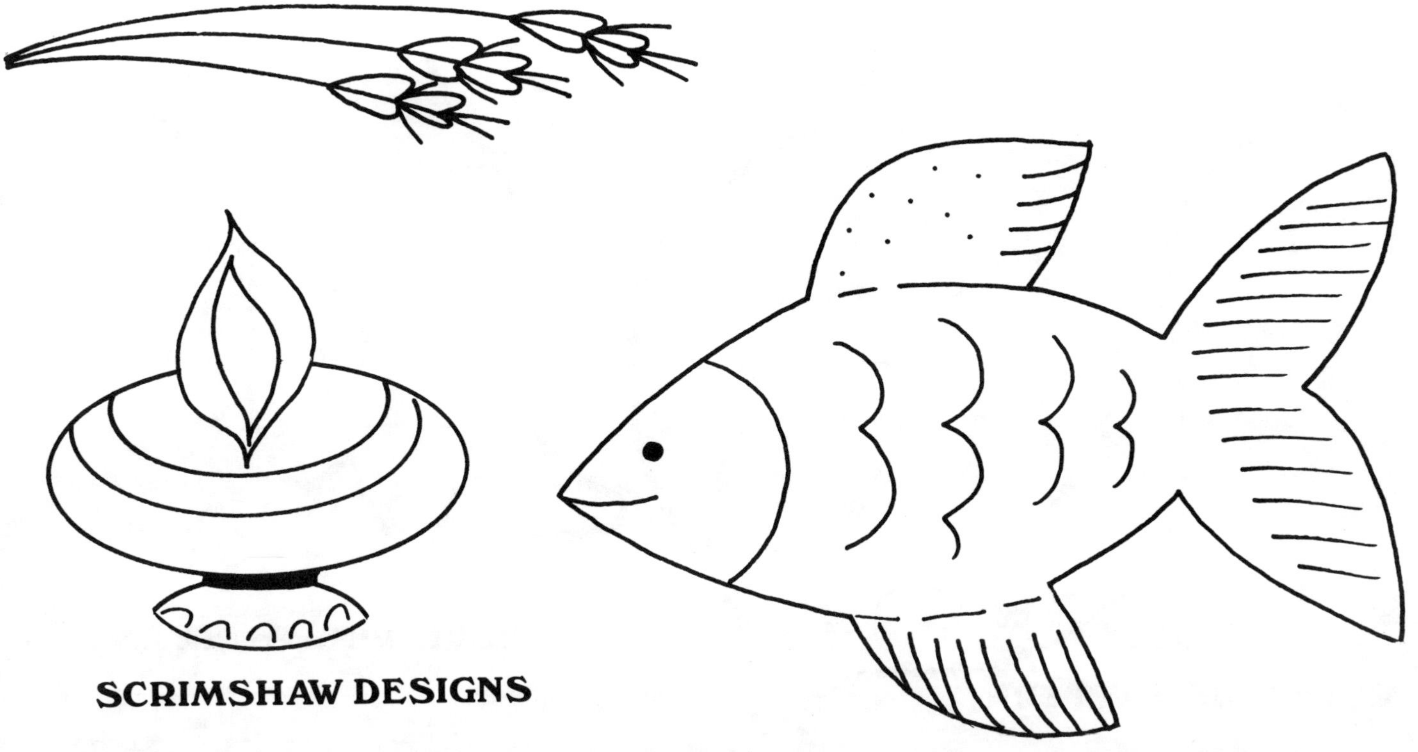

SCRIMSHAW DESIGNS

DOVE MOBILE

These easy-to-make paper birds will twirl and spin in summer breezes if you hang them in a window or outside. Reproduce the dove patterns on heavy white bond paper.

MATERIALS:

Heavy white bond paper
Dove patterns (three per mobile)
Scissors
String
1 coat hanger per mobile
Glue (optional)

DIRECTIONS:

1. Cut out bird pieces along heavy lines.
2. Fold on dotted lines and cut slits.
3. Fit pieces together as shown. Wings can be glued near slits for extra durability.
4. Hang string from two ends and middle of hanger as shown.

DOVE BODY PATTERN

DOVE WING PATTERN

WIND SOCKS

Hang these from trees outside the church to let the community know you're having Vacation Bible School. They remind passersby to be thankful for all God provides us in summer. Reproduce two patterns for each wind sock.

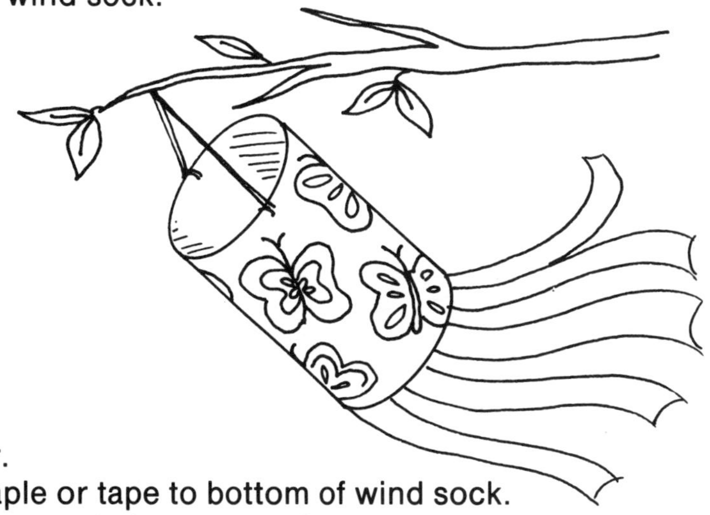

MATERIALS:

Wind sock patterns
5 crepe paper streamers cut in 36" lengths
Stapler or tape
Crayons or markers
String for hanging

DIRECTIONS:

1. Color the wind sock pieces.
2. Staple or tape together to make a cylinder.
3. Fold crepe paper streamers in half and staple or tape to bottom of wind sock.
4. Attach string to top and hang from a tree to catch the summer breezes.

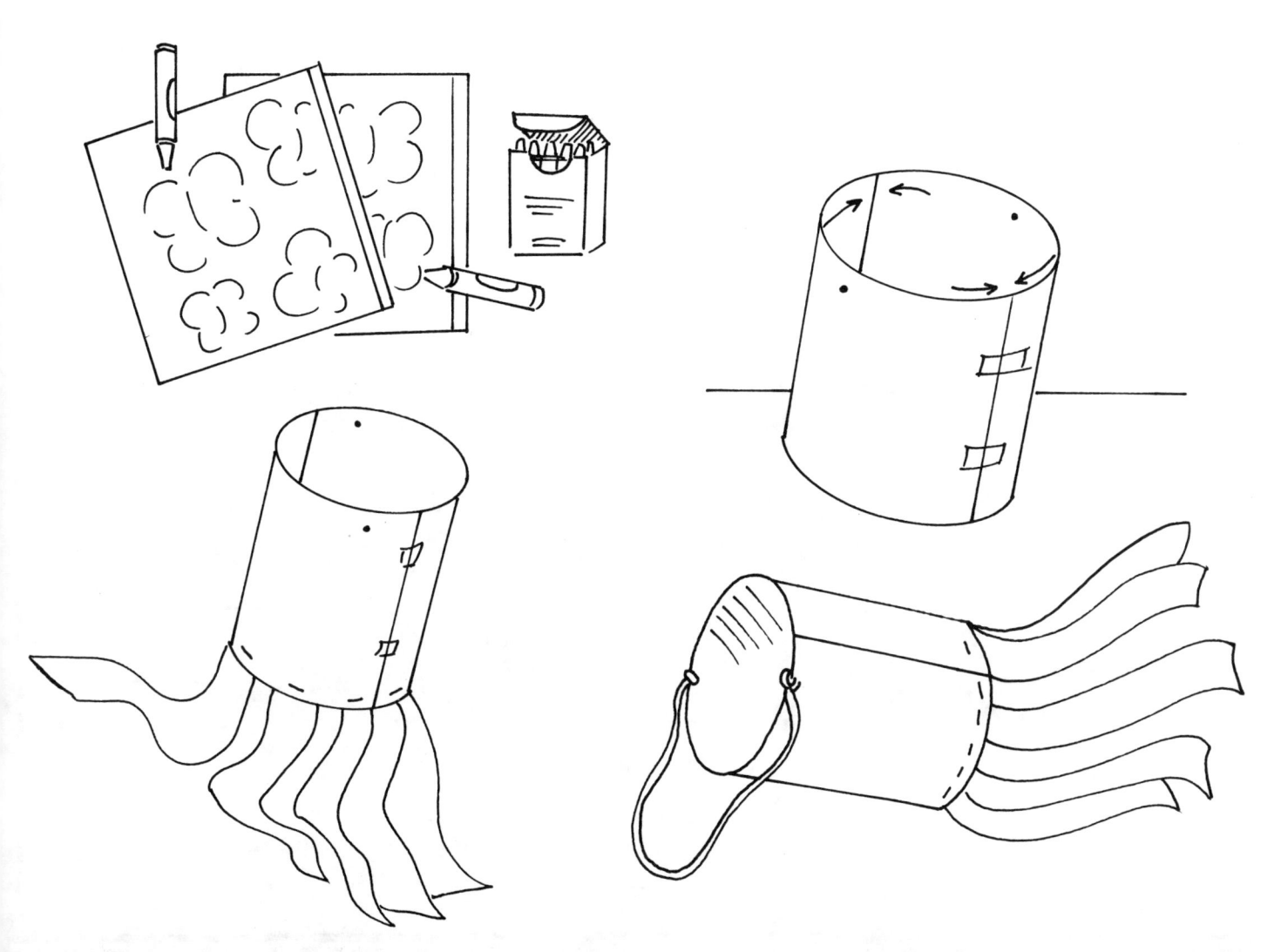

WIND SOCK PATTERNS

GLUE

GOD'S HELPER LITTER BAGS

Teaching children to take pride in their community is very important in God's plan for us. Reproduce the litter bag labels and badges on heavy tagboard. Promote community cleanup efforts by forming a "litter brigade" in your church neighborhood. The class can pick up any debris they find. Don't forget to recycle materials.

MATERIALS:

Litter bag label and badge
Crayons
Small plastic garbage bag
Glue
Safety pin
Heavy tagboard

DIRECTIONS:

1. Cut out litter bag label and badge.
2. Decorate with crayons.
3. Glue label to garbage bag.
4. Pin on your badge.
5. Use the bag to gather litter in your neighborhood or backyard.

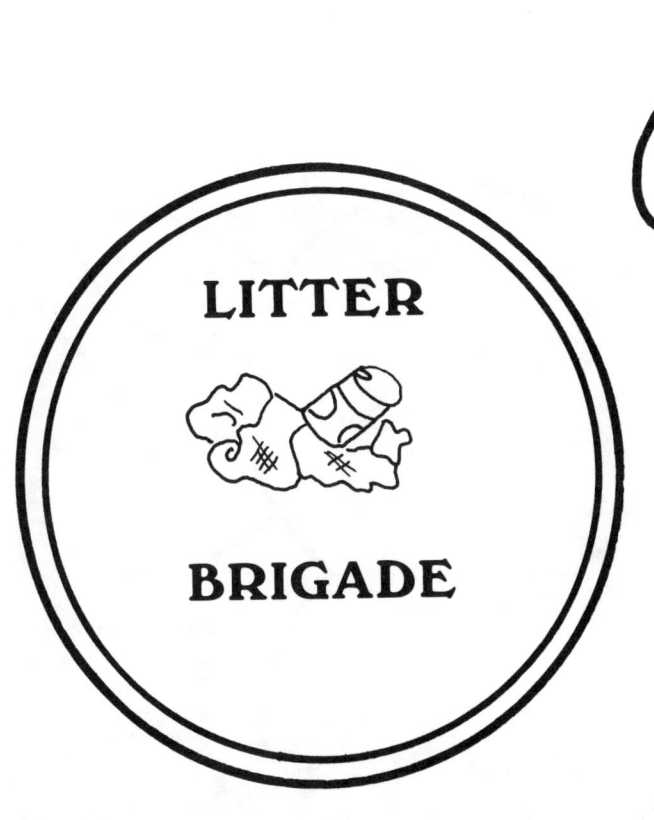

LITTER BRIGADE

KEEP GOD'S WORLD CLEAN!

LITTER BRIGADE

GROWING LOVE POSIES

Ask the children to make these flowerpots and posies for your church's shut-ins. They will make everyone feel needed and loved. Reproduce the flowers on pastel construction paper. The flowerpots can be reproduced on any color you have. Write your message on the stem and copy enough for each flowerpot.

MATERIALS:

Flowerpot pattern
Flower pattern
Flower stem with message
Scissors
Glue
Pastel construction paper

DIRECTIONS:

1. Cut out each piece.
2. Glue flower to top of stem with message face up.
3. Turn flower and stem face down. Glue bottom of stem inside the top of the flowerpot as shown.
4. Lightly fold up stem so that it is even with the bottom of the pot.
5. Fold flowerpot over stem. Fold down tabs and glue.
6. Send your flowerpot to a shut-in. He/She will pull the flower up to read your message of love.

GOD LOVES YOU!

BACK

FLOWERPOT PATTERN

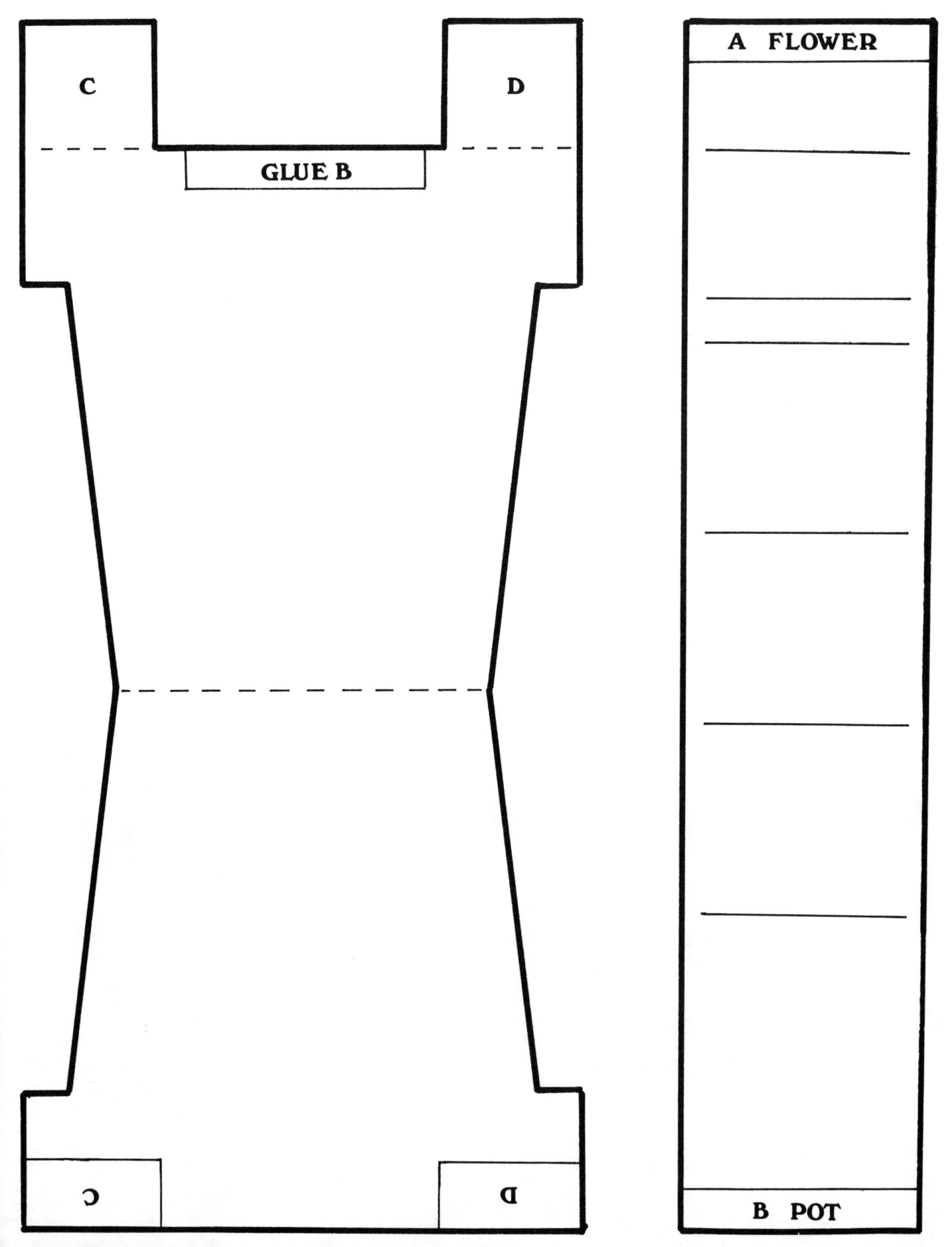

C D

GLUE B

A FLOWER

C D

B POT

SUN CAMERA "PHOTOS"

The sun will do most of the work in this outdoor project. It is best to use darker colors of construction paper that will fade quickly. Pick a day that's not too windy!

MATERIALS:

1 sheet dark construction paper
Various shaped leaves
1 sheet plain paper
Scissors

DIRECTIONS:

1. Cut a cross or some other shape you like from the plain paper.
2. Gather various shaped leaves outside and place them around the outside edge of the construction paper.
3. Place the cross or your special shape in the center of the paper.
4. Leave in the sun for about an hour.
5. Remove leaves and shape to reveal your sunshine "photo."

HOPPING BUNNIES RACE

Your bunnies will hop with joy! Reproduce on tagboard.

MATERIALS:

Hopping bunny pattern
Glue
Rubber band
Tagboard

DIRECTIONS:

1. Cut out bunny and ears. Glue ears in position as shown.
2. Fold on dotted lines and glue as shown.
3. Put rubber band around bunny body as shown.
4. To make your bunny hop, gently flatten with your hand and release quickly. After some practice you can have races with a friend.

LEAPING FROGS

Children love balloons. Hopefully, they'll leap for joy with a frog. Reproduce the pieces on green tagboard.

MATERIALS:

Frog head and feet
Scissors
Round balloon
Masking tape
Green tagboard

DIRECTIONS:

1. Cut out frog pieces. Cut slits in mouth.
2. Blow up balloon and knot.
3. Put knot through slits in head as shown. Position arms around balloon.
4. Tape feet onto balloon.

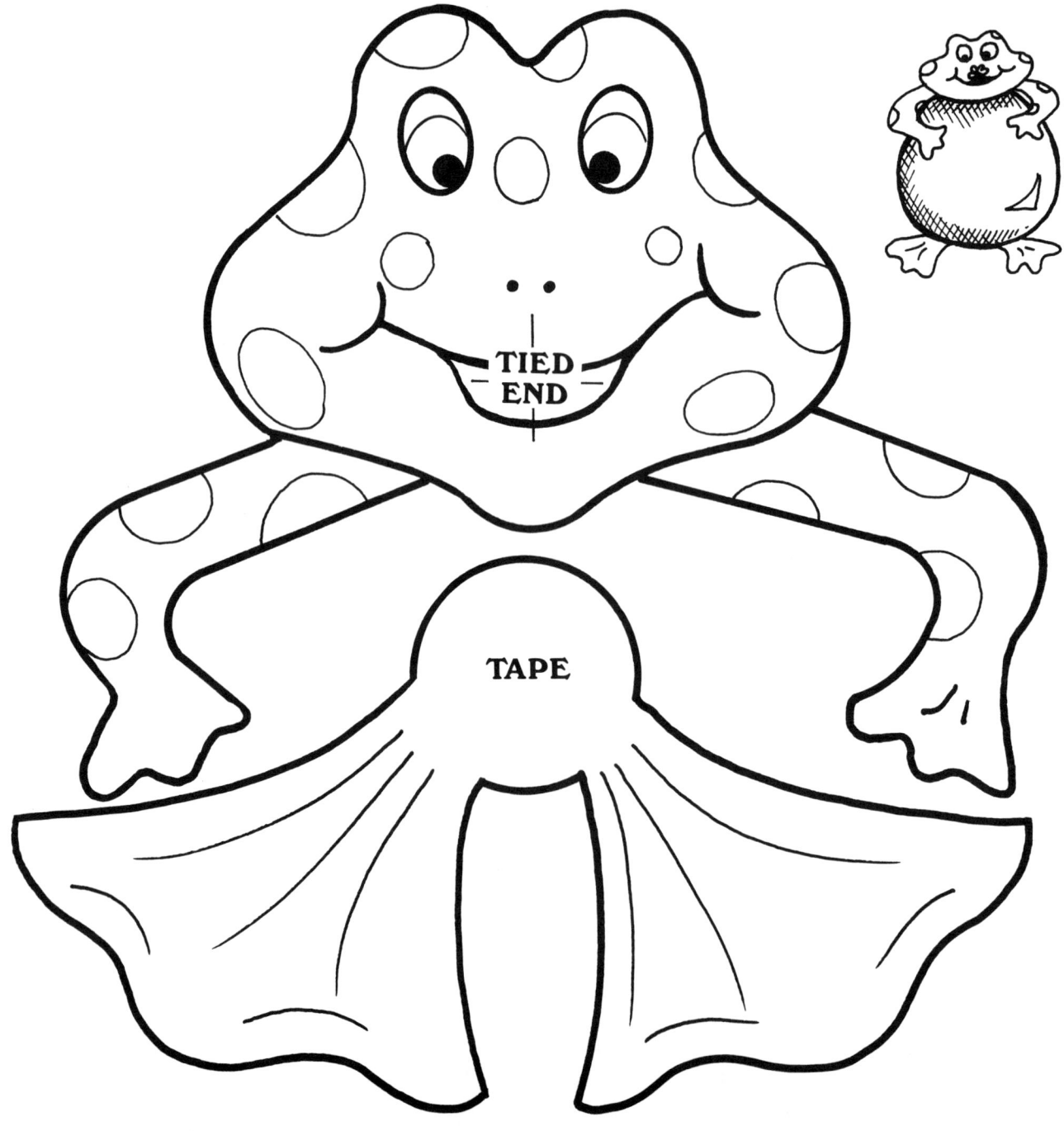

SUN CATCHERS

Even though the materials are quite simple, the results are really pretty. Cut the tissue into small pieces for easier handling. Children should not use the iron without very close supervision.

MATERIALS:

Waxed paper sandwich bag
Various colors of bright tissue paper
Scissors
Iron
Paper grocery bag

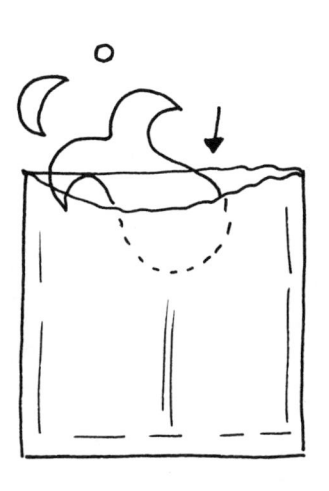

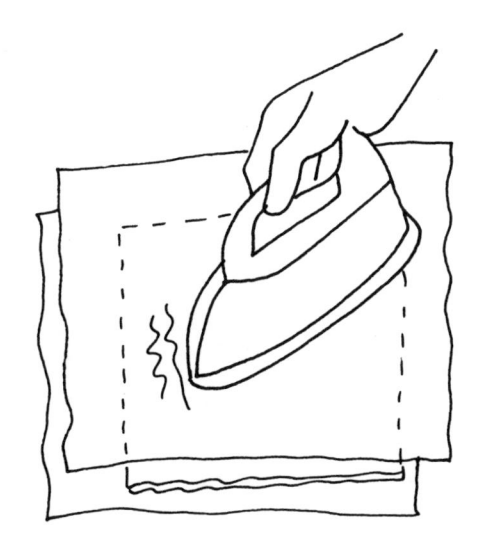

DIRECTIONS:

1. Cut tissue into pretty shapes and place in a single layer inside the sandwich bag.
2. Carefully place sandwich-bag picture between two sheets of grocery bag paper.
3. Press with a warm iron for a few seconds.
4. Remove sandwich-bag picture and hang in a window to catch the sunlight.

FUN TIME ROCK-A-LONGS

These little rockers show some of the ways children celebrate the gifts of summer. Copy on tagboard. Each child will need a base and one figure.

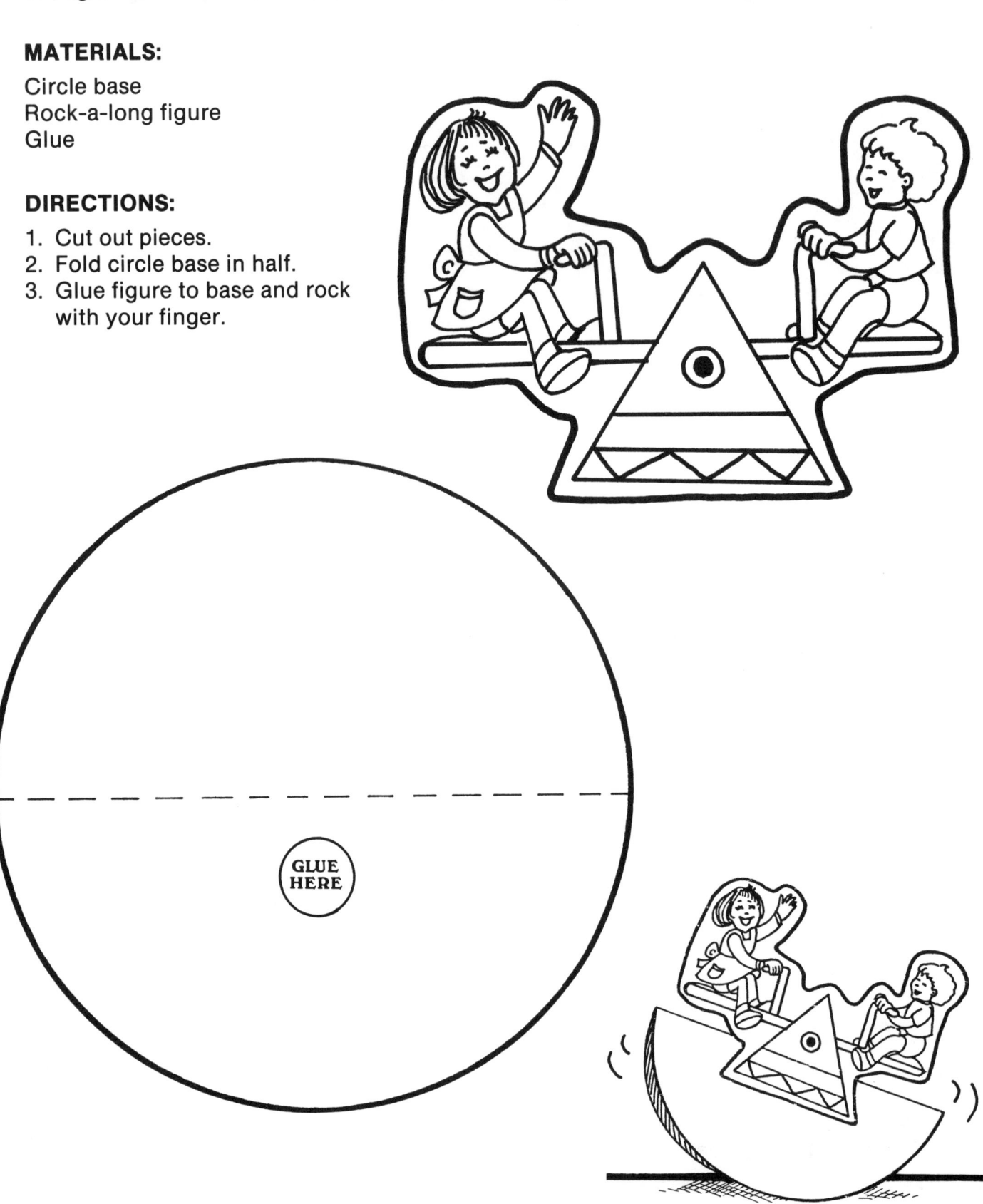

MATERIALS:

Circle base
Rock-a-long figure
Glue

DIRECTIONS:

1. Cut out pieces.
2. Fold circle base in half.
3. Glue figure to base and rock with your finger.

GLUE HERE

ROCK-A-LONG PATTERNS

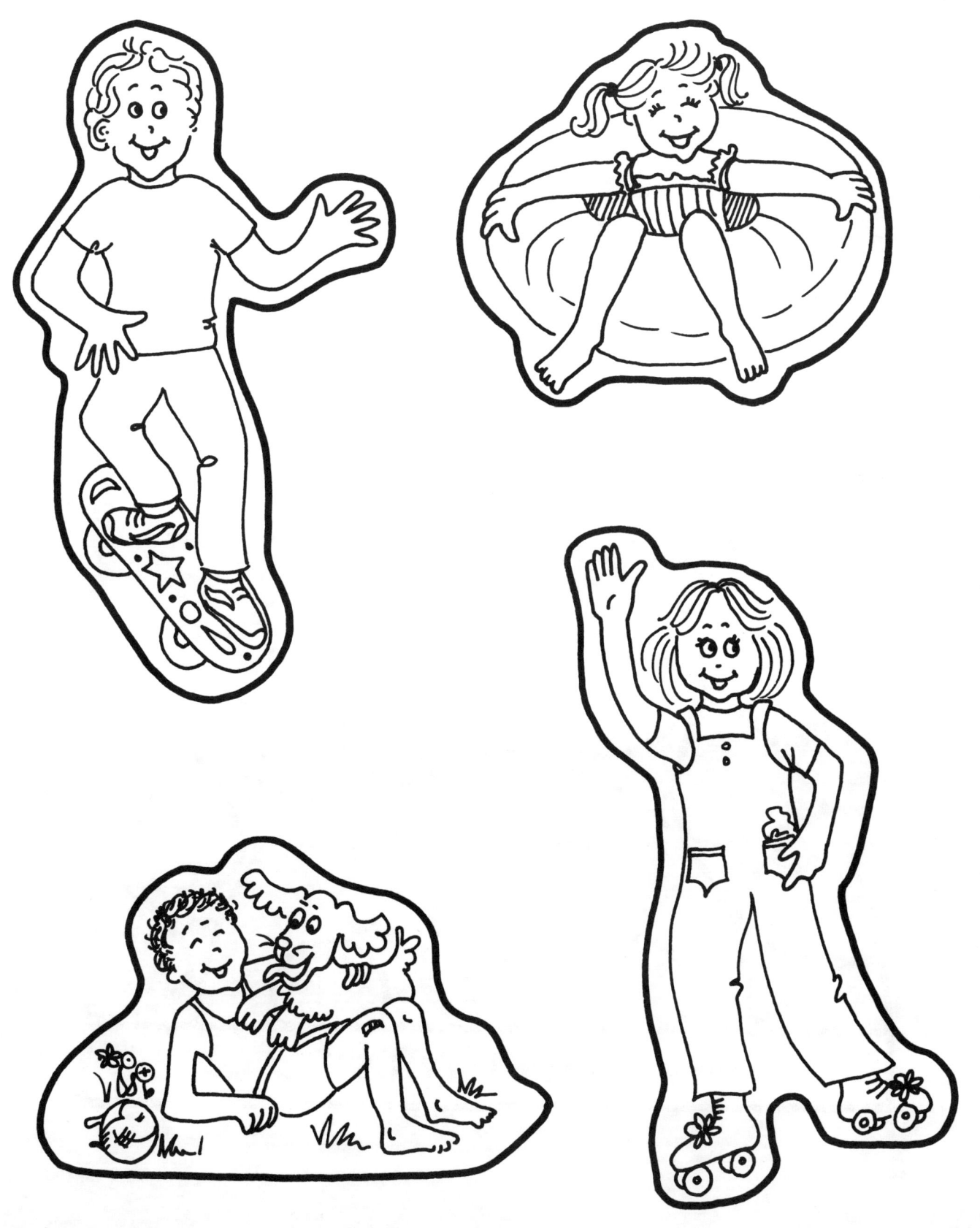

WEEKLY PRAYER FOLDER

A little pocket of prayers close to a child's pillow will help him/her remember to talk to God at bedtime. Copy a label for each folder. Cut off small tab. Fold up to one inch below center fold. You can write the prayers together or ask children to write their own.

MATERIALS:

Prayer label
File folder
Crayons (optional)
Masking tape
Glue

DIRECTIONS:

1. Fold and tape folder as shown.
2. Glue on label. Decorate folder if you like.
3. Write prayer reminders on the cards and tuck into pocket.
4. Slip flap under your mattress.
5. Use the cards each evening when you say your prayers.

MY PRAYER FOLDER

PRAYER CARDS

Reproduce on card stock.

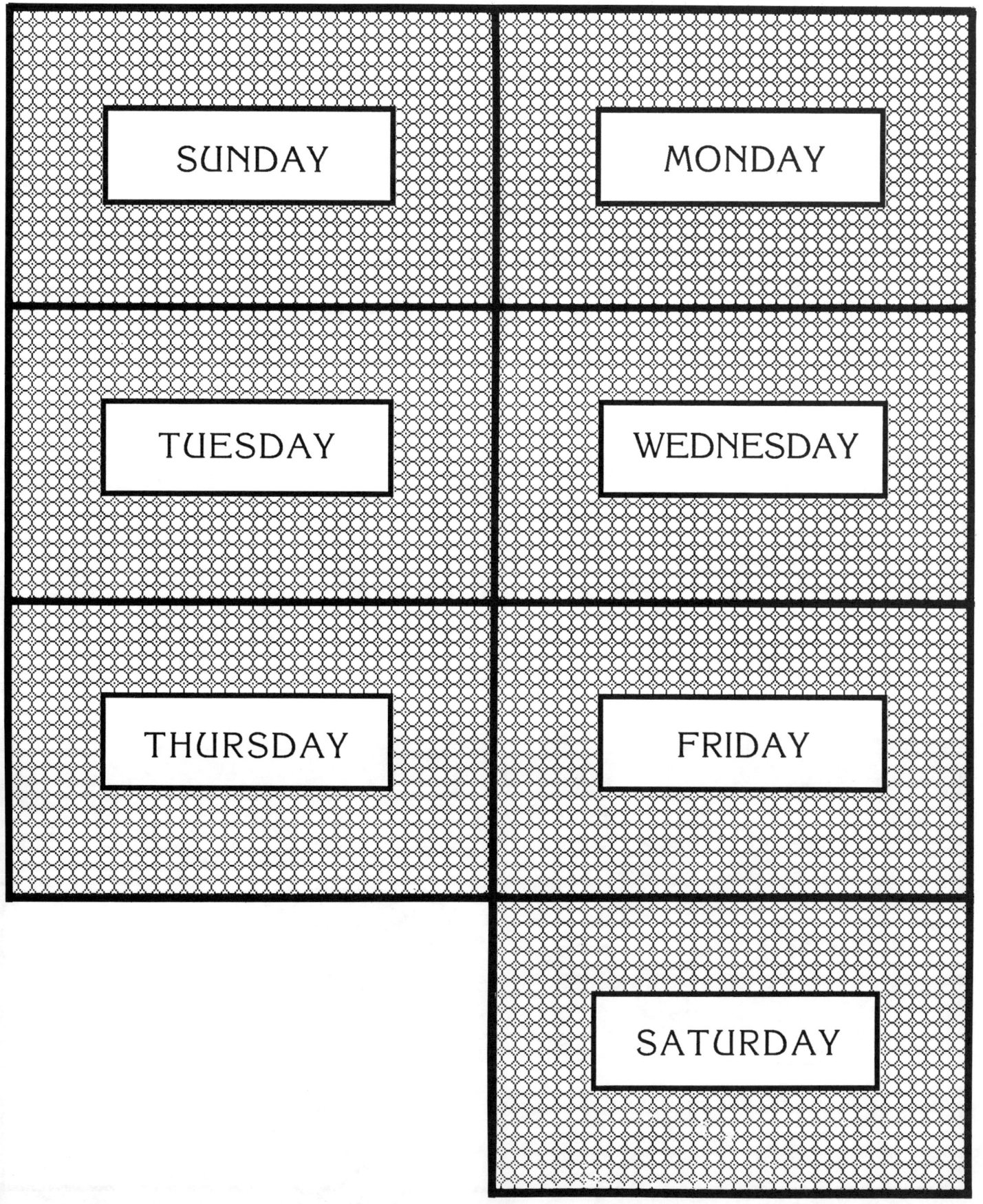

SUNDAY	MONDAY
TUESDAY	WEDNESDAY
THURSDAY	FRIDAY
	SATURDAY

BUBBLES UP AND AWAY!

Soap bubbles are fun on a warm summer day. Prepare the solution ahead of time; take everyone outside and enjoy!

MATERIALS:

Paper cup
Plastic straw
Bubble solution: ¼ cup dishwashing
   detergent, 2 cups water

DIRECTIONS:

1. Punch straw into bottom side of cup as shown.
2. Pour a small amount of solution into the cup.
3. Blow gently on the straw until bubbles foam out of cup and float away!

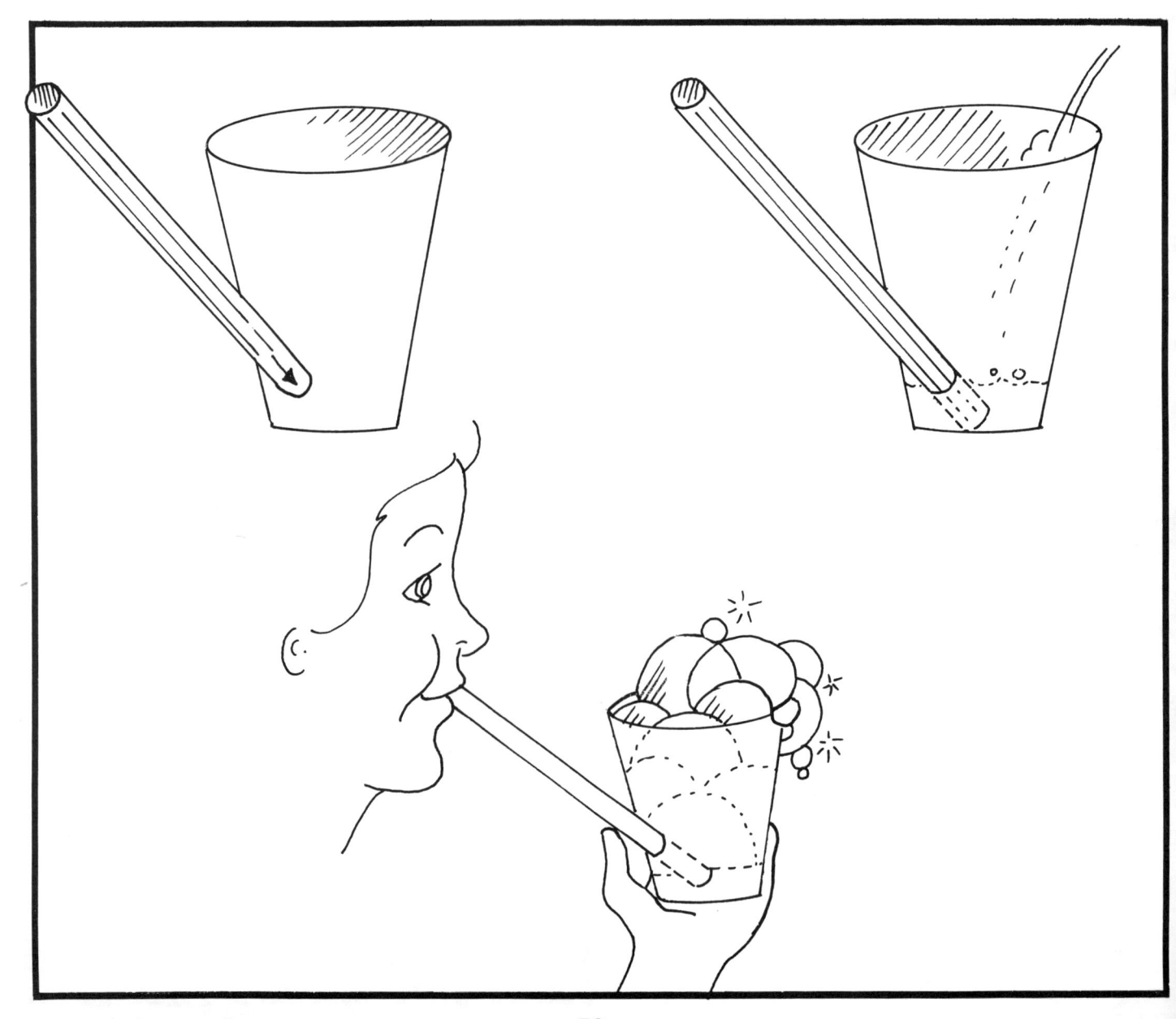

HEART SUN SPARKLERS

This is a nice, quiet activity to do outside on the grass. Copy the design on plain paper. Caution children not to look directly into the sun when they hold up their pictures.

MATERIALS:

½ sheet dark construction paper
Design sheet
Sharpened pencil

DIRECTIONS:

1. Place design on top of construction paper.
2. Use pencil to punch holes on dots through both sheets of paper.
3. Remove design sheet and hold your picture up to the sky to see the light come through. Do not look directly at the sun.

POP-UP GREETINGS

Your class may want to keep these cards for themselves, but it would be nice if they would send them to others. Reproduce on white card stock.

MATERIALS:

1 card and 1 pop-up
Crayons
Glue
White card stock

DIRECTIONS:

1. Color and cut out the pop-up and card.
2. Fold pop-up back on dotted line.
3. Fold card up on dotted line.
4. Glue pop-up tabs to card on circles.
5. Refold card and send to a friend.

POP-UP CARDS

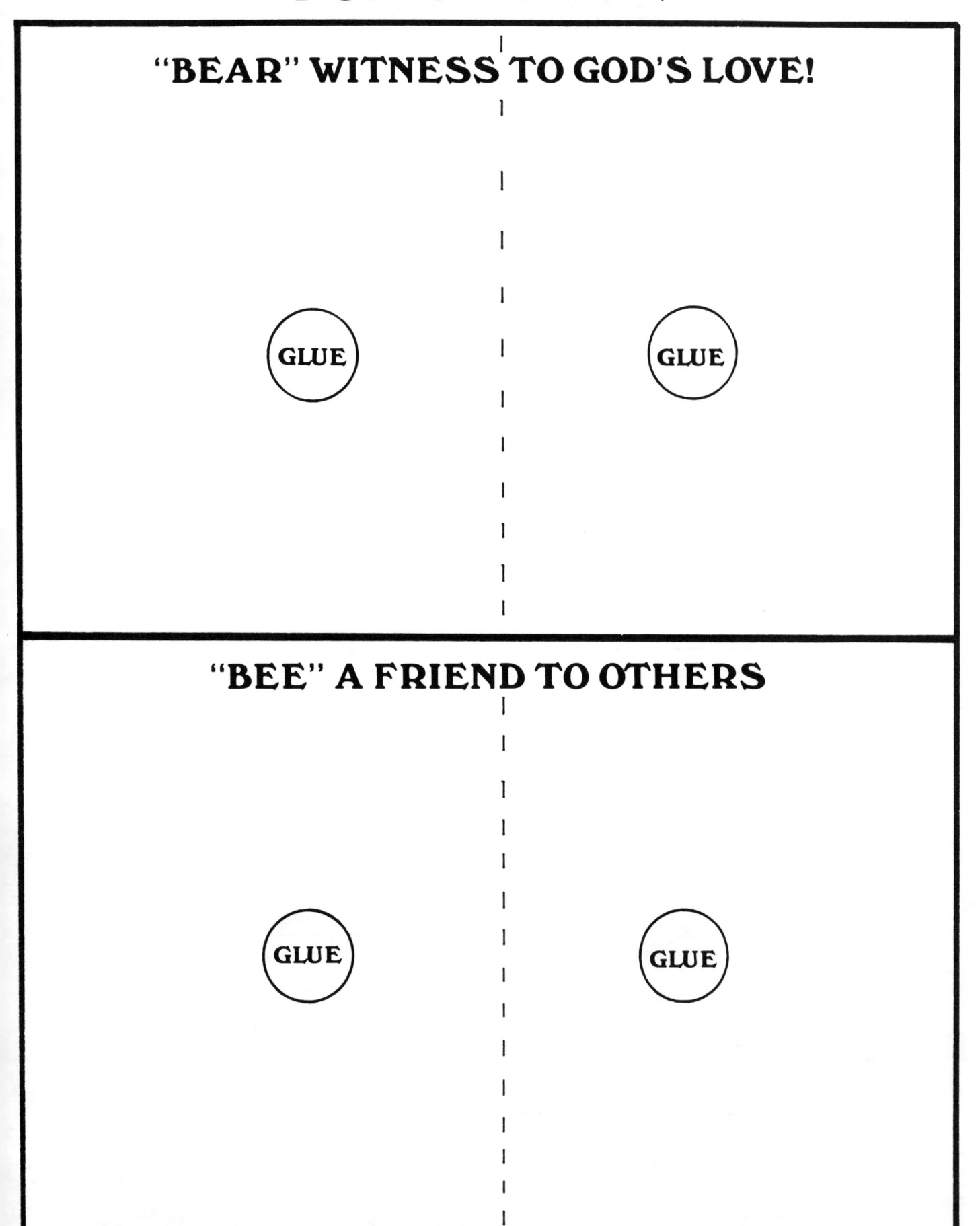

"BEAR" WITNESS TO GOD'S LOVE!

GLUE   GLUE

"BEE" A FRIEND TO OTHERS

GLUE   GLUE

"SANDY" PAINT

Take your class outside on a sunny day to paint. This paint has a shiny, grainy texture that looks like sand when dry. Have your students draw pictures of Jesus' homeland; then mix up some salt paint to fill in the desert areas. The rest of the picture can be painted with regular watercolors or colored with crayons or markers.

MATERIALS:

(For each child's portion)
Teaspoon, small bowl and paintbrush
2 teaspoons salt
1 teaspoon liquid starch
1 teaspoon water
A few drops of brown, gold or yellow
   tempera paint
Watercolors, markers or crayons
   (optional)

DIRECTIONS:

1. Draw desert scene.
2. Mix sandy paint in a small bowl in the color of your choice.
3. Paint the sandy areas, and set in the sun. When dry, color the rest of the picture with regular watercolors, crayons or markers.

SUNSHINY PAINT

Here is another special paint. It will look slick and shiny when dry. Have your children draw a picture of Moses in the bullrushes along the Nile, and paint the river with the slick paint. Or have the children plan stained glass window designs with simple shapes and Christian symbols. The outlines should be colored heavily with dark crayon and then the inside filled in with various colors of the sunshiny paints. Whatever the project, it will give a special glow to the students' artwork!

MATERIALS:

(For each child's portion)
Teaspoon
Small bowl
Paintbrush
White liquid glue
Tempera paint
Tagboard

DIRECTIONS:

Mix one part glue and one part paint in small bowl. Each child should make a small quantity of one color, then switch with other children to get a variety of colors. Allow paint to dry thoroughly before touching. Paint is best used right away before it dries. Any leftovers can be stored in airtight containers to prevent drying out.

GAMES
BIBLE SCHOOL CHANT

This little icebreaker is a simple way to let the children get acquainted. You can change the chant to suit different occasions. You may want to provide name tags if the children don't know each other.

Teacher (choosing a child):(name) touched the hem of Jesus' robe.
Child: Who me?
Class: Yes, you!
Child: Couldn't be!
Class: Then who?
Child: (names another person)
Class: (name) touched the hem of Jesus' robe.

(The chant continues until all have been named.)

RED ROVER OLD TESTAMENT GAME

Children will take an Old Testament name in this version of "Red Rover." Divide the class into two teams. Give each child a name tag to wear. The game is played in the usual manner. One team chants "Red Rover, Red Rover send (name) right over." That person runs over and tries to break through the clasped hands of the other team. If the runner breaks through, a player is chosen to go back to the other team. If the runner does not break through the line, he/she stays with the team. Teams take turns until allotted time runs out or there are no people left on one of the teams.

OLD TESTAMENT NAMES

Adam	Joseph	Eve	Delilah
Cain	Moses	Sarah	Ruth
Abel	Samson	Rebekah	Naomi
Noah	Samuel	Rachel	Hannah
Abraham	Saul	Leah	Michal
Isaac	David	Dinah	Abigail
Jacob	Solomon	Deborah	Esther

MOSES AT THE RED SEA BEANBAG TOSS

This game symbolizes the journey of the children of Israel from the Red Sea to Sinai. You can draw chalk lines and circles outside on the driveway for each stop along the way, or enlarge the symbols on page 59 with an overhead projector and place them on the floor. Circles should be about one foot in diameter and one foot apart. Follow the diagram below for setting up the game. Fill three old, clean socks with dried beans and sew securely.

Divide the group into two teams. Each team takes turns throwing the beanbags toward the circles. The child stands behind the Red Sea line and tosses the bags toward the circle, trying for the most points. Bags must be within the circle to score points. Keep tally of the points scored. The winners are the team with the most points after each child has had a turn.

- MARAH
- ELIM
- SIN
- HOREB
- SINAI

GAME SYMBOLS

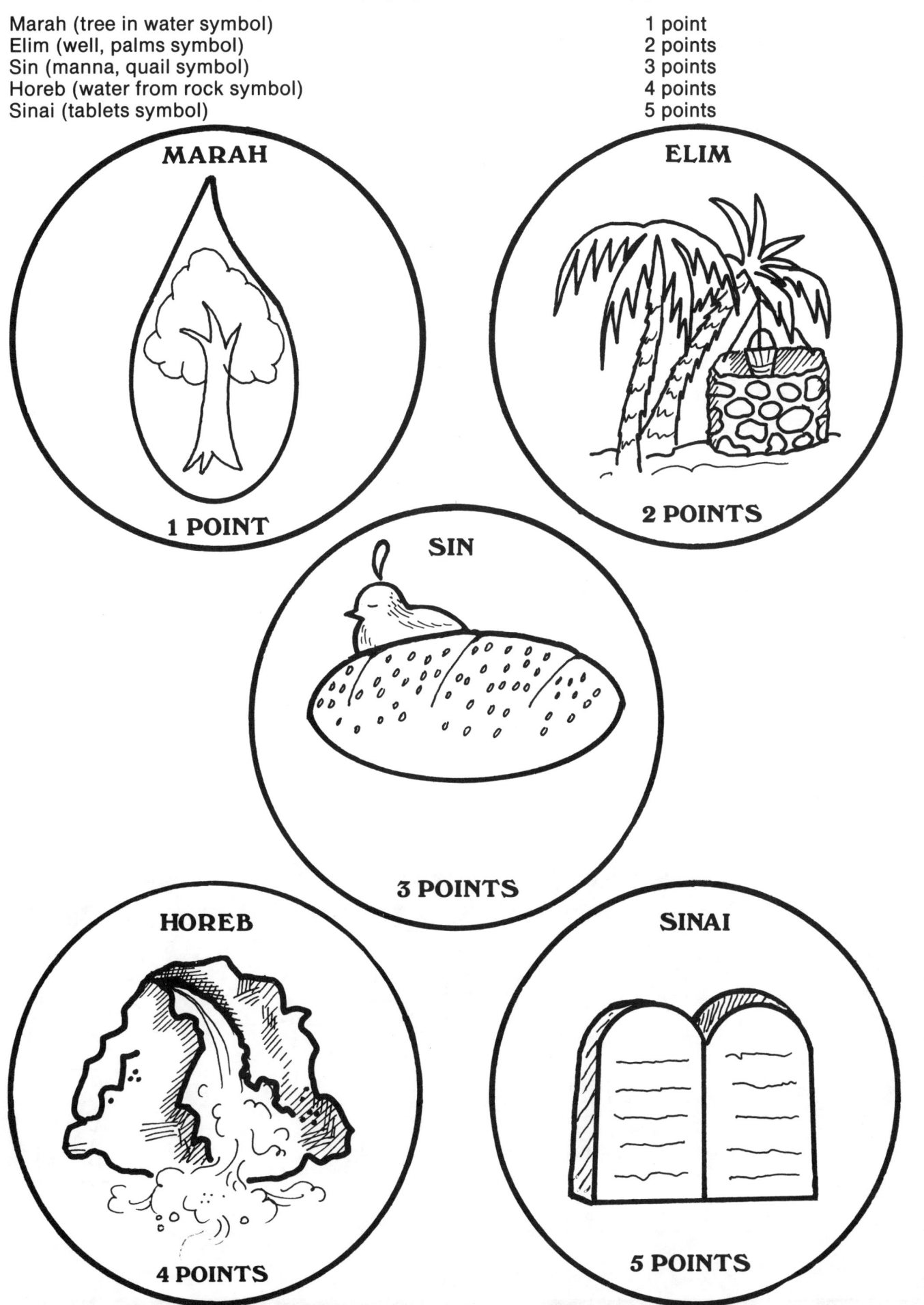

Marah (tree in water symbol) — 1 point
Elim (well, palms symbol) — 2 points
Sin (manna, quail symbol) — 3 points
Horeb (water from rock symbol) — 4 points
Sinai (tablets symbol) — 5 points

MARAH — 1 POINT

ELIM — 2 POINTS

SIN — 3 POINTS

HOREB — 4 POINTS

SINAI — 5 POINTS

DANIEL IN THE LION'S DEN

Your class can help Daniel stay away from the lion in this game. Children stand in a circle holding hands. One child is chosen to be Daniel and one to be the lion. The lion chases Daniel around the outside or inside the circle. The children in the circle raise or lower their arms to let Daniel pass between them or to keep the lion away from Daniel. When the lion tags Daniel, he becomes Daniel and a new lion is chosen.

WALL OF JERICHO

This is a safe tossing game. Fill ten large paper grocery bags with wadded-up newspapers, fold over and seal with masking tape as shown.

Stack nine of the bags (three rows of three) outside on the grass for the "wall." Each child gets a chance to be Joshua. As the rest of the children sing the chorus to the song, "Joshua" tosses the extra "stone" at the wall and tries to knock it down. You can keep score if you like, but it's fun for the children to play without scoring, too.

CHILDREN SING:

Joshua fought the battle of Jericho,
Jericho, Jericho.
Joshua fought the battle of Jericho
And the walls came tumbling down!

LEAP FROG

Children use the balloon frogs in the craft section (page 44) for a race outside on the grass. Children line up in a row with their frogs. On your signal they kneel on the grass and start to blow their frogs across the lawn. The first child to reach the finish line is the winner.

JORDAN RIVER REGATTA

You'll need a small wading pool for this game. Use the Styrofoam pool toys (page 29) for a race across the river Jordan. Several children try to blow their toys across the pool. The first to reach the other side wins.

NOAH'S ARK CHARADES

GAME ONE:

Copy the ark on the following page, color and attach to egg carton as shown. Fill the ark with all sorts of animal names written on slips of paper. Divide the children into teams of three or four members each. During each team's turn, a child picks an animal from the ark and has thirty seconds to act like that animal as team members try to guess the animal. If they guess the animal, the team gets to keep the animal card. After all the teams have had a chance to play five times, the team with the most animal cards wins.

GAME TWO:

Copy the ark and cut in half on the dotted line. You'll need one ark half for each child. Write the name of a different animal on each ark. Place the arks in a circle on the floor or grass. The teacher or a designated child is "Noah." While singing or listening to music, children march along from ark to ark. On Noah's signal the children stop. Noah names one child to imitate the animal on his/her ark. The other children guess the animal. If the children guess the animal correctly, the designated child becomes the new Noah and the game continues.

NOAH'S ARK PATTERN

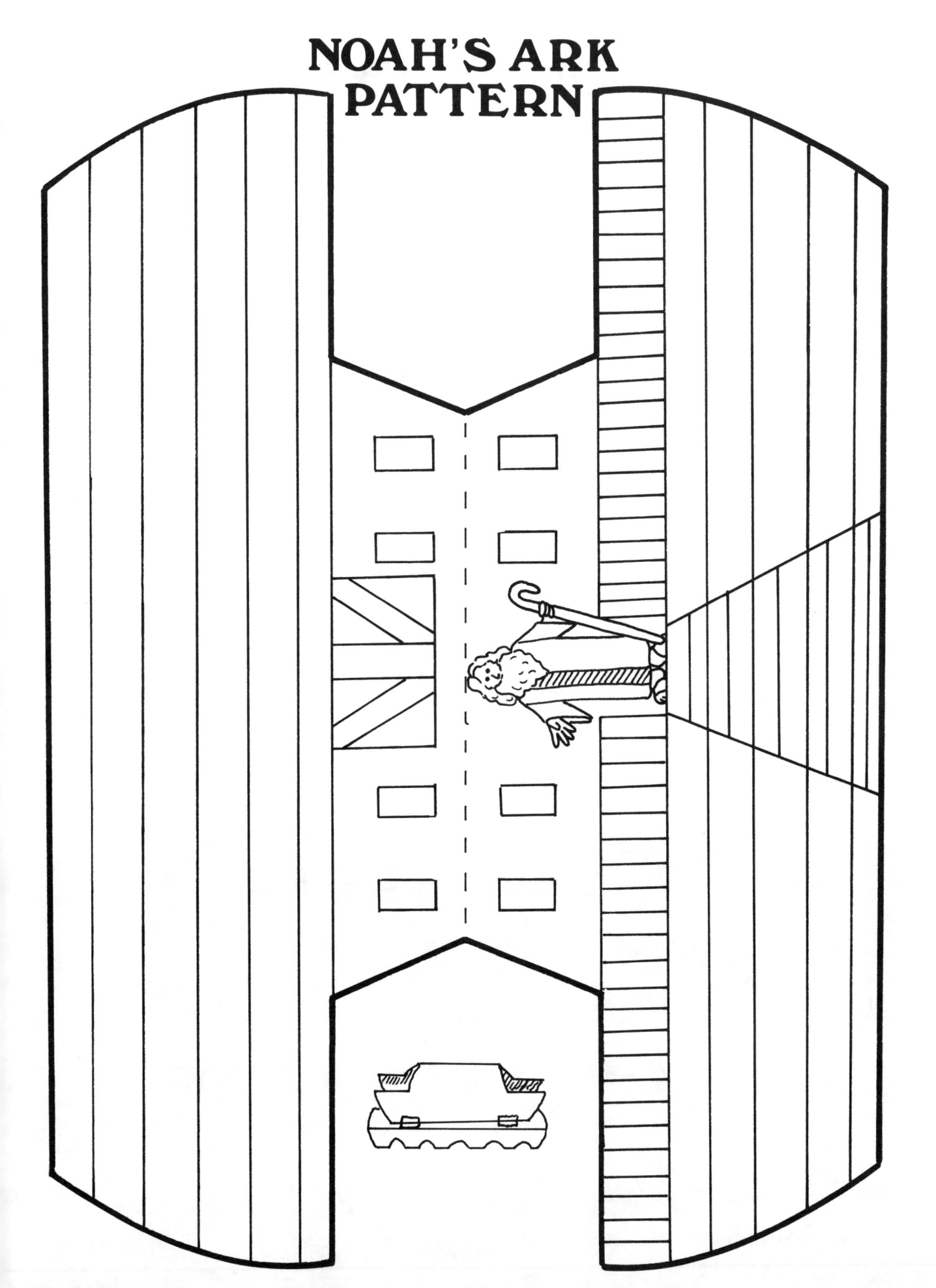

63

Shining Star Publications, Copyright © 1989, A division of Good Apple, Inc.

SS1813

CAMEL TAG

In this game children pair up to be a "camel" and its "hump." The humps place their hands on the camels' shoulders. An extra player (the camel rider) tries to catch onto the shoulders of the hump. If there are an even number playing, there are two camel riders. The camels run around to keep the riders from grabbing the hump. If the driver is successful, the camel drops away and becomes a camel driver. The hump becomes the camel, and the camel driver becomes the hump as play continues.

CAMEL

"HUMP"

CAMEL RIDER

OUTDOOR BOARD GAME

(for 4 to 8 players)

Cut out lots of footprints for an outdoor "board" game with children as the playing pieces. On a third of the footprints, write the penalty and reward phrases listed below. Place all the footprints in a winding path outside. Make a big paper-bag "die" as on page 61. Add numbers to the sides with a marker. Children pair up for teams. One person tosses the die while the partner moves the number of spaces along the path. Players follow directions on the footprint they land on. If one lands on a PARTNERS CHANGE footprint, the team partners exchange positions. The first team to reach FINISH wins.

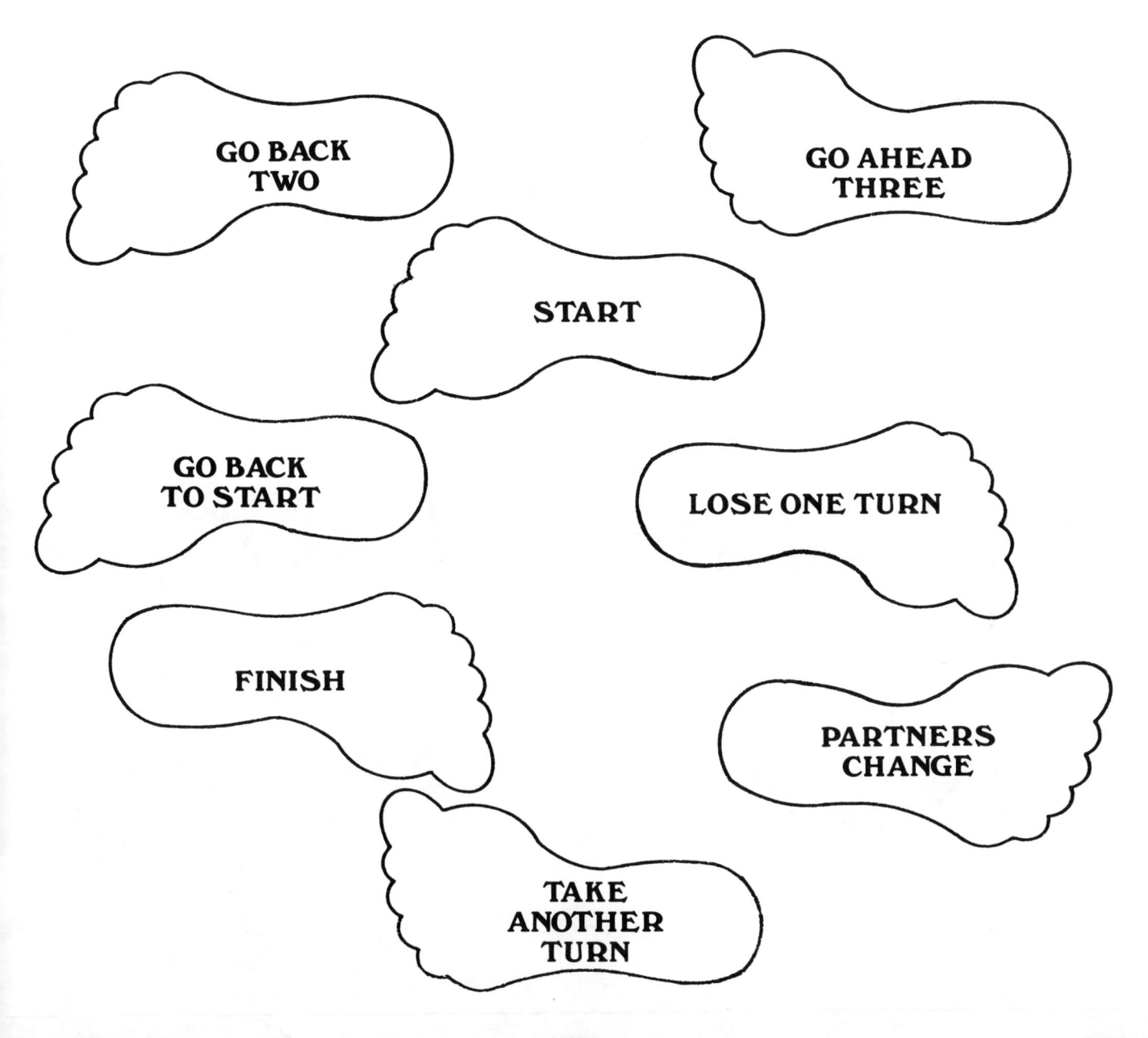

GO BACK TWO

GO AHEAD THREE

START

GO BACK TO START

LOSE ONE TURN

FINISH

PARTNERS CHANGE

TAKE ANOTHER TURN

FOOTPRINT PATTERNS

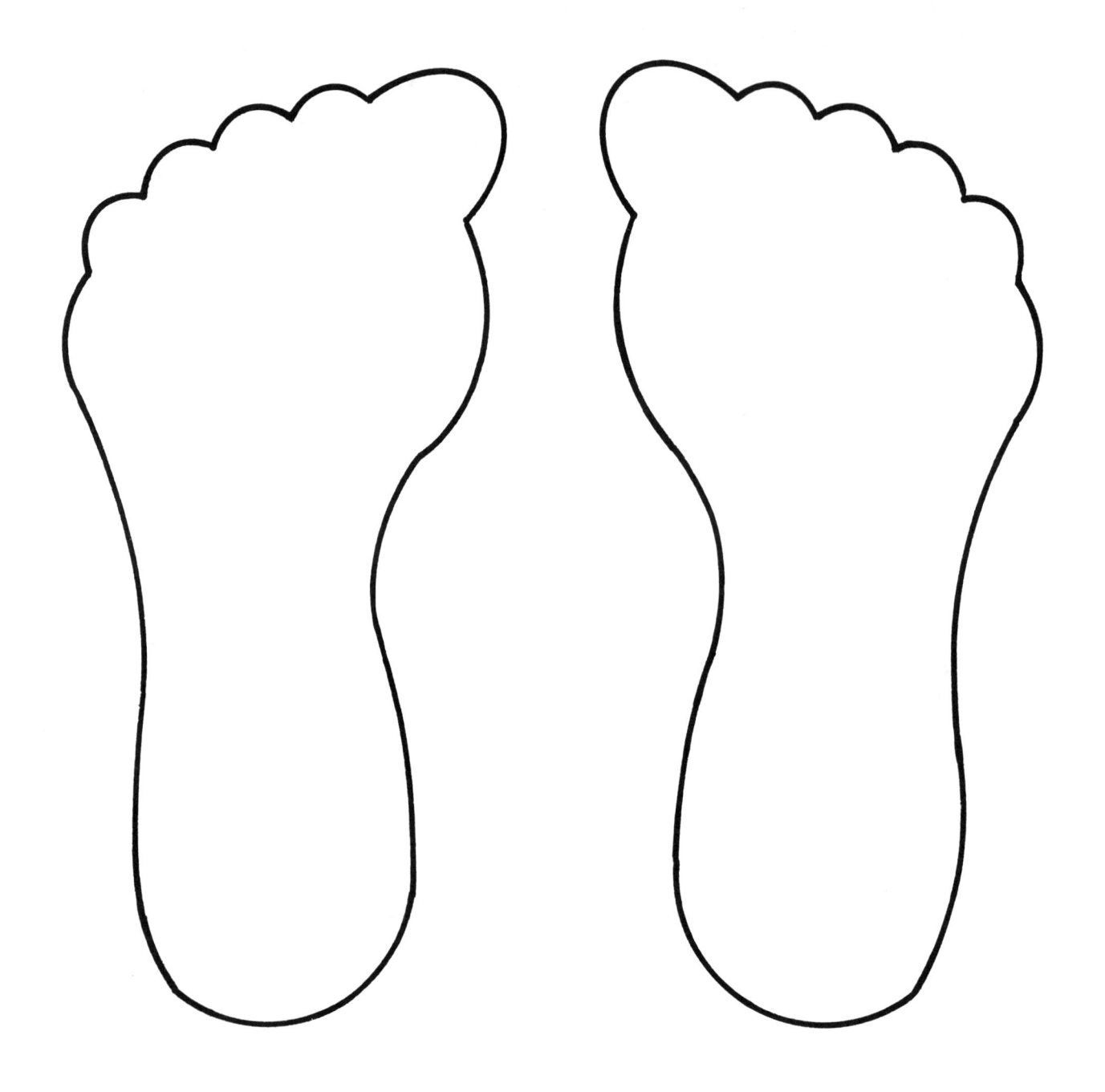

JUMP OVER JORDAN GAME

Cut two lengths of clothesline rope about four feet long. Lay them out parallel on the ground, as shown, about two feet apart (narrower for younger players). Children line up and jump over Jordan without touching the ropes. If a child misses, he/she is out of the game. Make the river wider each time the children jump. The player who can jump the widest river is the winner.

VACATION BIBLE SCHOOL FIELD DAY

You can build all the relay games on the following pages into one big event for the closing of your Bible School program. Older children can help set up the games and younger ones can make the prizes. There should be supervision for each game. Each class goes through the various games together. Ideas for setting up each game are provided. This is a great way for all the children and teachers to participate and work together to plan a fun day for everyone. Each child who wins an event gets a paper token prize that is placed on a yarn "necklace." You may want to plan refreshments for all those thirsty marathoners at the end of the events. The games work well by themselves if you don't plan a field day, but they should all be played outside. Choose the games that are appropriate for your age group.

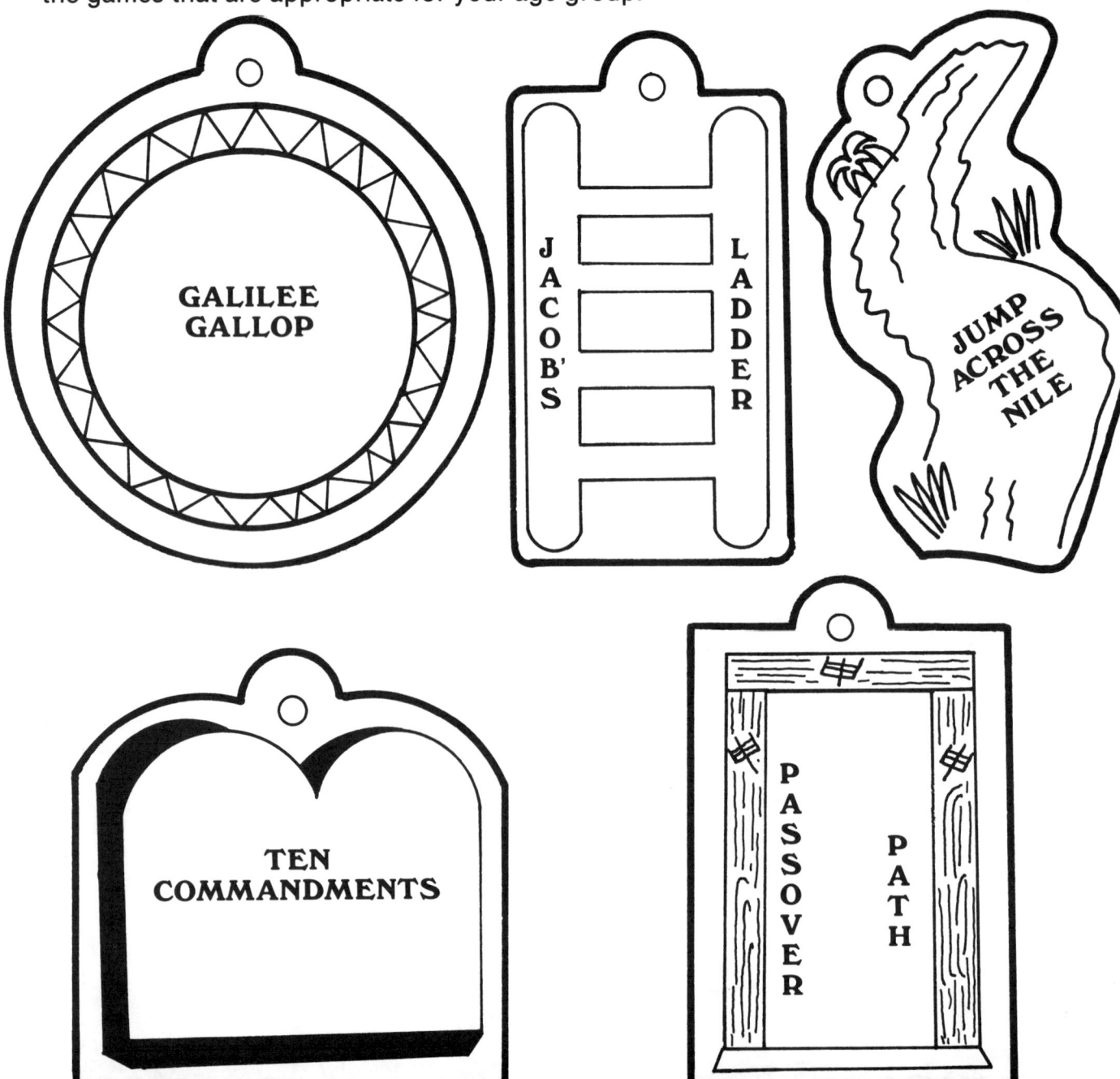

GALILEE GALLOP

JACOB'S LADDER

JUMP ACROSS THE NILE

TEN COMMANDMENTS

PASSOVER PATH

OBSTACLE COURSES

This takes up a lot of room, but is fun for the children. Use household items or chairs for children to move over, around, under and through to get to the end of the course. If your church has a playground, you can incorporate those items in your course. Children can pass slower children in this game. Each child who completes a section gets a token.

1. **JOSEPH'S JUMP ACROSS THE NILE:** Place two pieces of rope about three to four feet apart. Children must jump across the Nile without getting "wet."

2. **GALILEE GALLOP:** Arrange hula hoops as shown or draw chalk circles on the driveway. Children must hop into each hula hoop.

3. **JACOB'S LADDER:** Use a long ladder. Children tiptoe between the rungs.

4. **PASSOVER PATH:** Paint red symbols on "doors" made from grocery boxes. Children jump over the doors. If they miss, they must start again.

5. **TEN COMMANDMENTS MAZE:** Use ten large appliance or food boxes placed in a winding course. Each box has the number and the commandment pasted to it. Children crawl through the boxes in the proper order before going on.

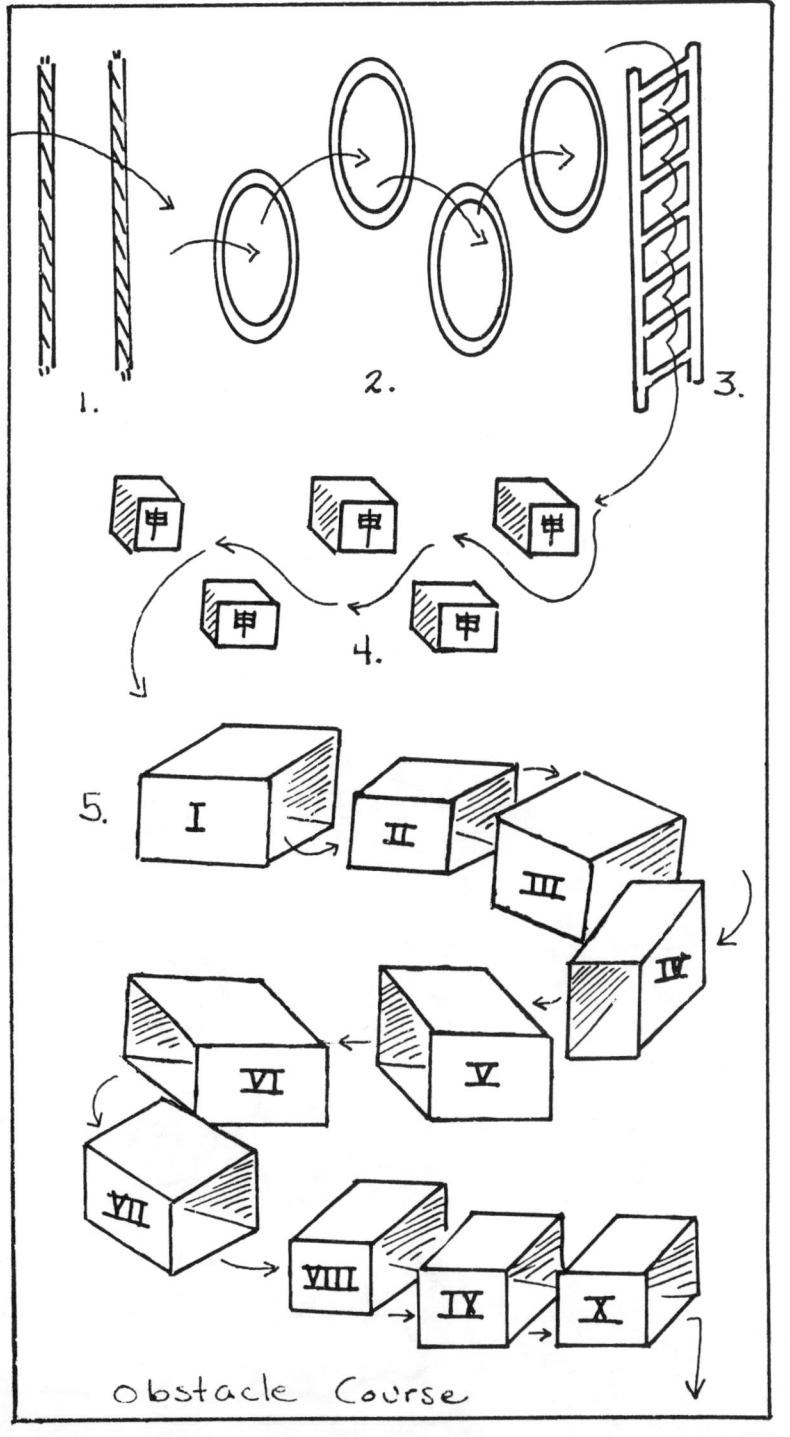

OVER THE MOUNTAINS AND UNDER THE SKY RELAY

Divide children into teams of six or seven players. Each team will need a beanbag. Children line up behind the leader of each team. The leader passes the beanbag over his/her head to the next player, who passes the bag between the legs to the next. Play continues "over the mountains and under the sky" to the last player and back to the leader. The first team to finish wins. Each member of the winning team gets a mountain token for his/her necklace.

OVER   **UNDER**   **OVER**

MOUNTAINS-SKY RELAY

MANNA RACE

Staple the lips of two sturdy paper plates together to form "manna" loaves. There should be one loaf for each child on each team. Children divide into four or five teams. Stacks of manna for each team are placed at the opposite end of the playing area. On your signal the first player on each team runs to the stack and takes one manna loaf and runs back to his/her team. The second player takes that manna loaf, runs back to the stack, picks up a second and runs back with both loaves. The third child takes the two loaves, runs back to the stack, gets a loaf and runs back to the team with three loaves. If a child drops the loaves of manna, he/she stops to pick them up before continuing. The first team to retrieve all their loaves wins and gets a manna token.

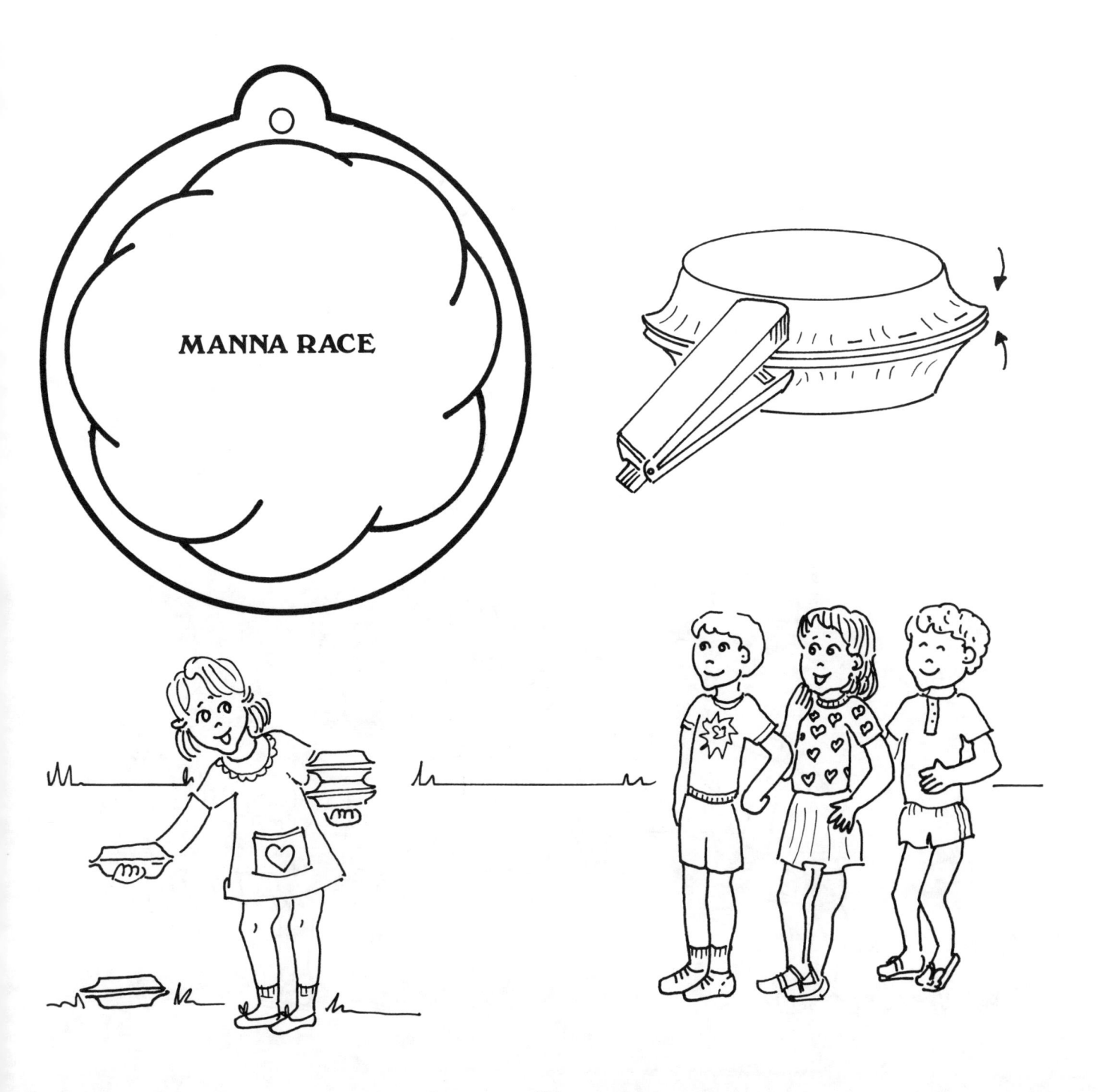

PHARAOH'S GOBLET RACE

Each team will need two pails and a paper coffee cup (the kind with handles). Each team lines up next to a pail of water. The first player dips the cup (goblet) into the water then walks or runs to the end of the field and pours the water into the team's empty pail. He/She runs back and gives the empty cup to the next player, who dips the cup in the pail and runs to empty the water. The first finished or the team that has the most water in their pail at the pre-arranged time for the end of the race wins a goblet token.

DELIVER GRAIN TO JOSEPH'S GRANARY

Divide children into teams of five or six. One person (Joseph) on each team sits on the ground at the end of the playing area. Use disposable pie plates for Joseph's hats. Punch holes on two sides and string with yarn so that the pie plate sits on top of the head. Each team is given a large serving spoon and a bag of roasted peanuts in the shell. On your signal the first person on each team scoops peanuts into the spoon and walks or runs to Joseph and dumps the peanuts into the pie plate. Joseph must sit very still to keep the peanuts in his hat. If a child drops peanuts along the way, he/she cannot stop to pick them up. The team that has the most peanuts at the end of the race is the winner. Each winning member gets a Joseph's granary token.

SNACKS

FRIGID FROSTIES

Children can make these outside. They're fun, frosty and nutritious!

Large plastic Ziploc bag
Ice
Hammer

Put ice in plastic bag. Seal bag and crush ice with the hammer. You'll need ½ cup ice per cooler. Small groups of children can take turns doing this part of the recipe. When everything is ready, bring out the rest of the ingredients and let each child make his/her own frosty.

TO MAKE ONE COOLER:
½ cup crushed ice
1 sandwich-size Ziploc bag
1 plastic straw
2 tablespoons frozen fruit juice concentrate, thawed (any flavor)
½ cup milk
1 scoop vanilla ice cream

Put ice, milk, juice concentrate and ice cream into sandwich bag. Zip the bag closed and mix with fingers. Open one end of bag, slip in straw and reclose. You can sip your Frigid Frosty right from your mixing "bowl"!

WATERMELON FIZZ

4 cups seeded, chilled watermelon
1 large bottle ginger ale, chilled
Ice cubes (optional)

Place 1/3 cup watermelon in a 7-ounce paper cup. Crush with a spoon. Add ice and ginger ale. Slurp away!

BLUEBERRY BUBBLES

An adult should be in charge of the blender. Children can add their own blueberries.

2 cups blueberries
4 cups milk
¼ cup sugar or honey

Put milk, sugar or honey and one cup of blueberries into blender. Blend until smooth. Pour into six cups. Float a few blueberries on top. Drink with a straw or let the blueberry bubbles tickle your nose!

FRUITY SUN TEA

1-16 oz. can pineapple chunks
1 jar maraschino cherries
Orange segments
2 family-size tea bags
Gallon jar
Water

Place fruit and juice in jar. Add water to fill. Add tea bags and cover. Set out in the sun for two hours. Remove tea bags and serve over ice.

A PAPER CUP FOR EMERGENCIES

When you're outside or away from home and need a quick drink, you can make a paper cup from notebook paper.

DIRECTIONS:

1. Cut paper into a 7½-inch square.
2. Fold paper into a triangle.
3. With crease at the bottom, fold left corner to the center of the right side.
4. Fold right corner to left side in the same manner.
5. Fold top corners down over each side.
6. Open up your cup and pour!

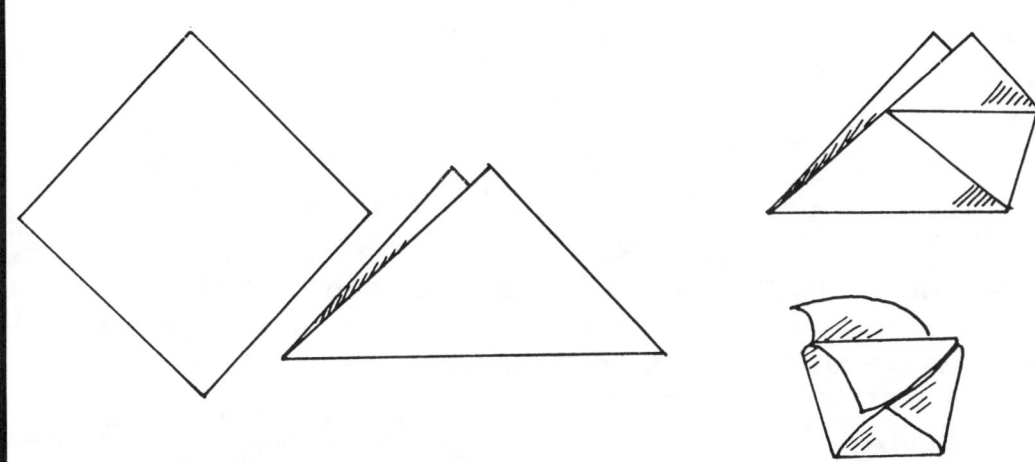

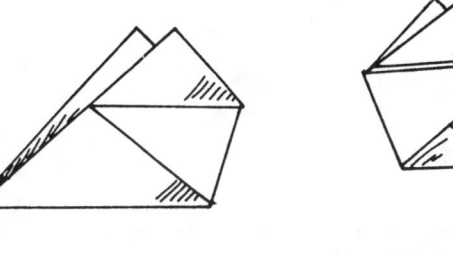

LOAVES AND FISHES SNACK

This is very simple and symbolic of Jesus' miracle.

2 cups Ritz Bits crackers
2 cups Pepperidge Farm goldfish crackers
1 cup golden raisins
1 package (6 oz.) semisweet chocolate chips (optional)

Mix all together in a large bowl. Makes about seven cups.

BUMPS ON A LOG

Children can make these themselves if you have plastic knives for them to use.

1 bunch celery
Peanut butter or cream cheese
Raisins

Break the celery into stalks. Wash each stalk and cut off the top and the bottom. Fill celery stalks with peanut butter or cream cheese. Stick a few raisins in the peanut butter. Cut into serving size pieces.

PEANUT BUTTER CLAY

Mix, create and eat!

1 cup peanut butter
1 cup corn syrup
1½ cups nonfat dry milk
1¼ cups powdered sugar
Raisins and pretzel sticks for garnish

Mix first four ingredients into a clay consistency. Add a little more dry milk, if it seems too sticky. Give each child about one-quarter cup "clay." Allow children to create anything they like. Place bowls of raisins and pretzel sticks in the center of the table for children to use for decoration. Makes over four cups of clay.

SUNBURST SANDWICHES

Get all the ingredients together, then let the children make their own sunshiny creations (after they have washed their hands). Amounts will depend on the size of the group.

Whipped cream cheese
Sliced canned pineapple
Grated carrots
Raisins
Toasted English muffin halves

Mix a little juice from the canned pineapple into the cream cheese to make of spreading consistency. Give each child a toasted muffin half. The rest of the ingredients should be in bowls in the center of the table. Spread the muffins with cream cheese mixture. Sprinkle carrots around the outside edge to make "sun rays." Top with a pineapple slice and decorate with raisins. Enjoy!

SONGS
SUMMERTIME FUN FINGER PLAY

(Sung to the tune of "The Wheels on the Bus")

MOVEMENT: Children move their arms over their heads in a big circle.

The sun in the sky shines bright all day.
bright all day,
bright all day.
The sun in the sky shines bright all day.
Summertime is here!

MOVEMENT: Children make hands look like hungry baby birds, touching fingers to thumbs.

The birds in the trees go peep, peep, peep,
peep, peep, peep,
peep, peep, peep.
The birds in the trees go peep, peep, peep.
Summertime is here!

MOVEMENT: Children squat down, puff out cheeks, and bounce up and down.

The frogs in the pond go croak, croak, croak,
croak, croak, croak,
croak, croak, croak.
The frogs in the pond go croak, croak, croak.
Summertime is here!

MOVEMENT: Children hold their shoulders tightly and shiver and shake.

The kids at the beach say, "Too cold to swim,"
"Too cold to swim,"
"Too cold to swim."
The kids at the beach say, "Too cold to swim."
Summertime is here!

MOVEMENT: Children can pretend to swing a bat or throw or catch a ball.

The kids at the park say, "Let's play ball,"
"Let's play ball,"
"Let's play ball."
The kids at the park say, "Let's play ball."
Summertime is here!

I CAN LISTEN TO MY JESUS

(Sung to the tune of "I've Been Working on the Railroad")

VERSE 1:
I can listen to my Jesus,
I can learn to pray.
I can learn to love my neighbor
Each and every day.

Jesus has given me the answer,
If I only look.
All I need to know to love Him
Is written in His book.

REFRAIN:
It's written in His book, if I only look.
All I need to know is in His book.
It's written in His book, if I only look.
Everything is in His book.

VERSE 2:
I can listen to my Jesus;
I can learn to love,
I can learn to help another,
Help comes from above.

Jesus has given me the answer,
If I only look.
All I need to know to love him
Is written in His book!

REFRAIN:
It's written in His book, if I only look.
All I need to know is in His book.
It's written in His book, if I only look
Everything is in His book.

GOD'S GARDEN

(Sung to the tune of "On Top of Old Smoky")

Fluffy caterpillars and tiny green snakes,
Bright orange geraniums, tomatoes on stakes.

Prickly cucumbers with long leafy vines,
Big round watermelons that will taste just fine.

Dozens of daisies are all in a row,
Pounds of poppies are starting to grow.

Billions of butterflies flutter and swoosh,
Bunches of beetles eat my broccoli bush.

Zillions of zucchini I must pick each day,
Pecks of green peppers pop out of the clay.

Legions of lilies sway in the breeze,
Mountains of marigolds make me sneeze!

The sun gives it life as the rains give it food;
God's garden is rich now, God's garden is good!

JOY SONG AND FINGER PLAY

Use this little poem to get little ones up and moving after a quiet work time.

I've got a joyful feeling;
It starts down at my toes; (wiggle toes)
It makes my kneecaps jiggle; (shake legs)
It makes my shoulders go (shrug shoulders).

It makes my fingers snappy; (snap fingers)
My hands reach to the sky; (hands up in the air)
Joy makes me feel so happy; (arms out at sides)
I feel like I could fly (flap arms at side)!

BUDDY SONG AND DANCE

(Sung to the tune of "Twinkle, Twinkle, Little Star")

MOVEMENT: Pair the children off; one is the leader, the other the buddy.

BOTH SING:
Be my buddy,
Dance with me,
But you must look so carefully.

MOVEMENT: Both children hold hands and skip in a circle while leader sings.

LEADER SINGS:
If I touch my knees like this,

MOVEMENT: Leader touches knees, buddy follows suit.

LEADER SINGS:
Just be sure you do not miss.

MOVEMENT: Children skip in circle again.

BOTH SING:
Be my buddy,
Dance with me,
But you must look so carefully.

MOVEMENT: As song is sung, leader does movement, while buddy follows.

LEADER SINGS:
I can stand like a soldier straight,
Or bend and twist in a figure eight,
Squat down low,
Climb up high,
Swim and swim,
Or fly and fly.

MOVEMENT: Children skip in circle again.

BOTH SING:
Be my buddy,
Dance with me,
But you must look so carefully.

NOTE: At this point partners can switch places or exchange partners to dance another round.

PUPPETS
BIBLE STORY PLAYERS AND THEATER

These stage and stick puppets can be many characters for the Bible stories you tell to the class. The children can put on their own plays, too.

Reproduce each piece on tagboard, color and cut out. Assemble theater as shown in diagram.

BIBLE STORY THEATER

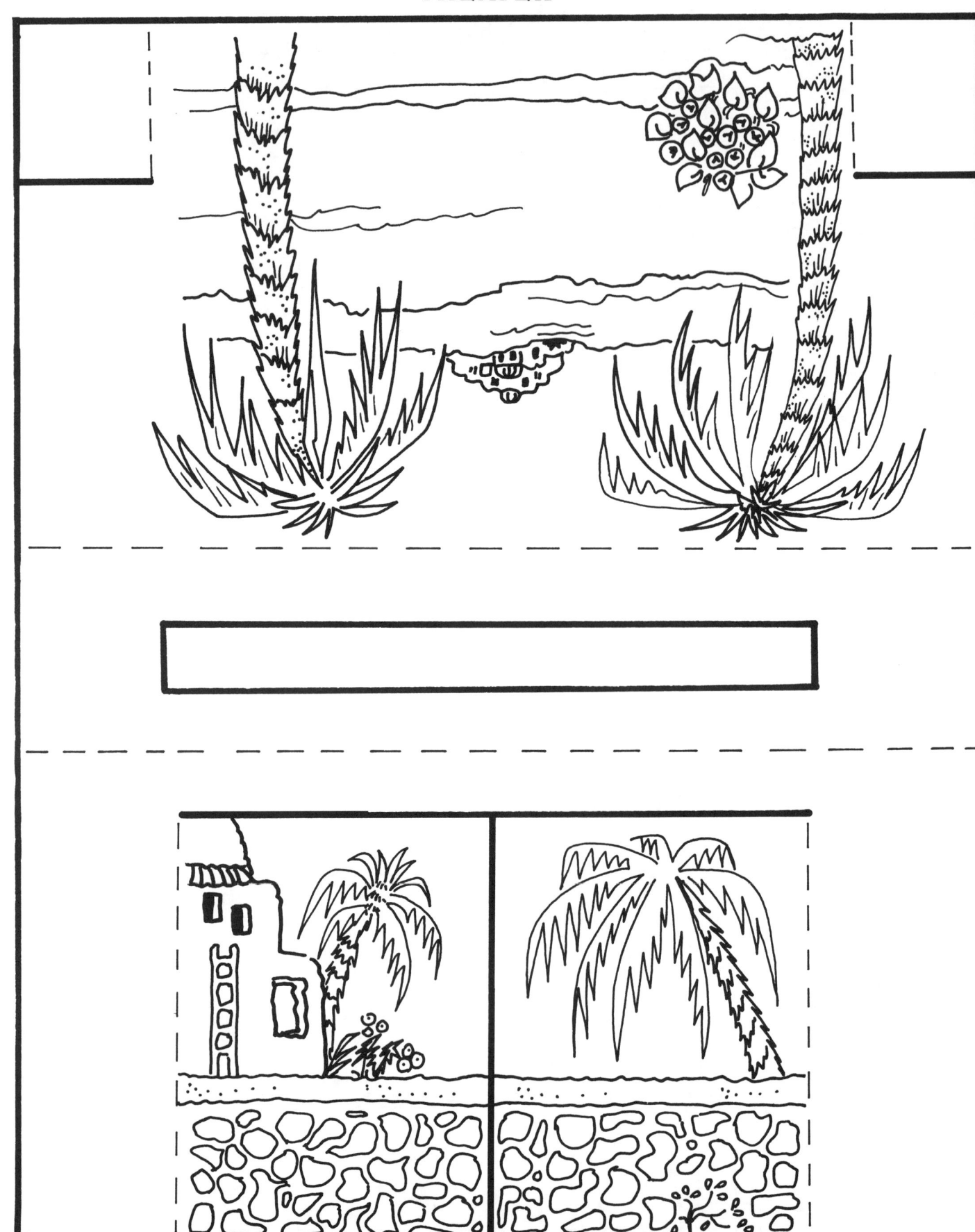

BIBLE STORY PLAYERS

MARY BABY JESUS

KING

JESUS

BIBLE STORY PLAYERS

ANGEL

SOLDIER

JOSEPH

BIBLE STORY PLAYERS

MARY
WOMAN
GIRL

SHEPHERD
APOSTLE
SAMARITAN

PHARAOH
PRIEST
SICK MAN

PUPPETS IN A CUP

Puppets with short poems remind children of some of the things God wants them to do. Copy all on white paper.

MATERIALS:

7-ounce paper cup for each puppet
Puppet
Cup cover
Scissors
Crayons or markers
Glue
Tape
Pencil

DIRECTIONS:

1. Color and cut out each piece.
2. Glue cup cover to cup.
3. Push pointed end of pencil up through bottom of cup.
4. Tape puppet to pointed end of pencil.
5. Move puppet up and down as you read the poem.

CARING KITTEN
Caring Kitten likes to share.
And a picnic is just the way
She shows her friends
That she cares.
How will you share today?

PUPPY LOVE

WELCOME

PUPPY LOVE

WELCOME

PUPPY LOVE
Puppy Love likes to be at home.
It's his favorite place to play.
When he's done, he picks up
All his toys.
Because helping is God's way.

GLUE

Shining Star Publications, Copyright © 1989, A division of Good Apple, Inc.

87

SS1813

LITTLE MOUSE

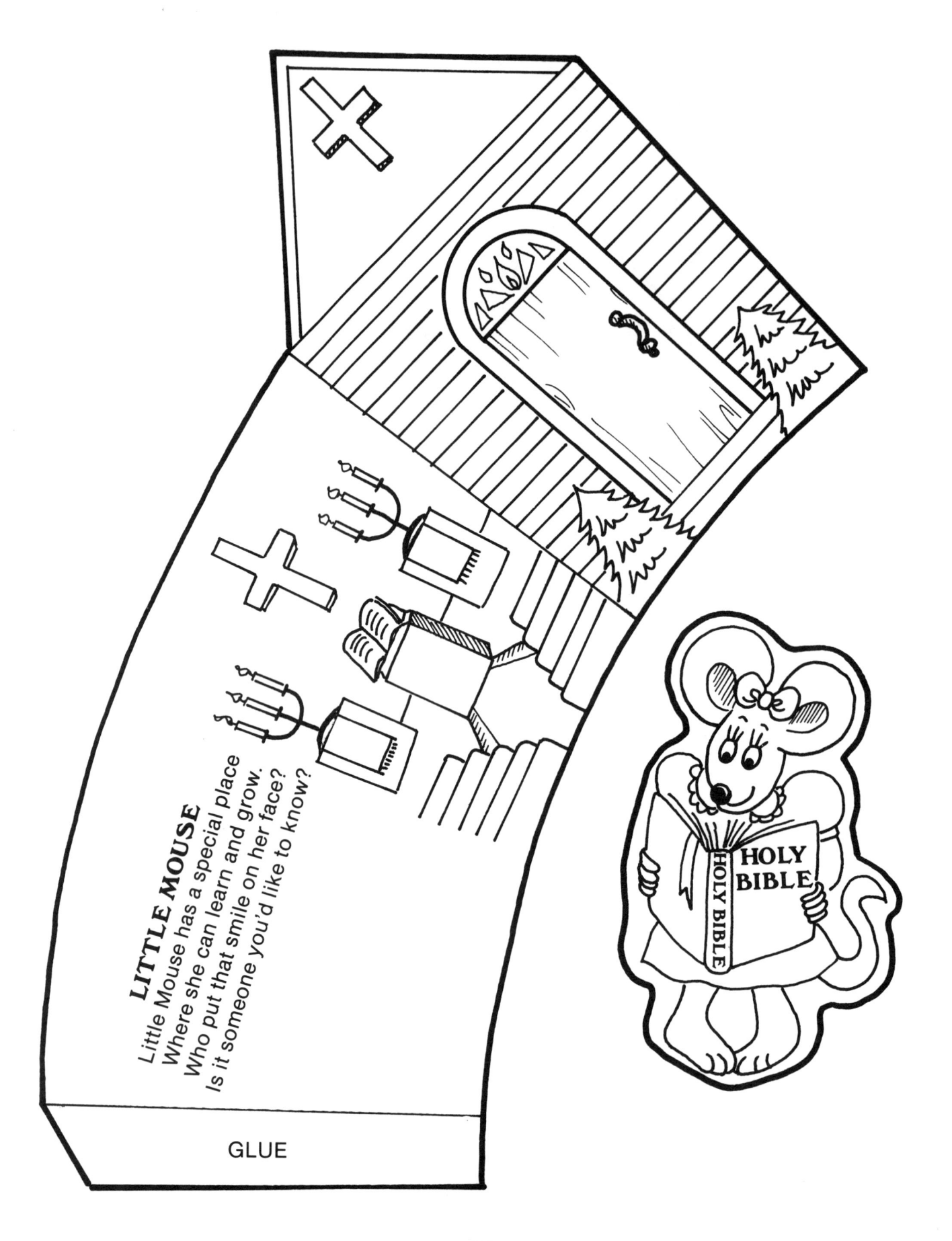

Little Mouse has a special place
Where she can learn and grow.
Who put that smile on her face?
Is it someone you'd like to know?

GLUE

CARING KITTEN

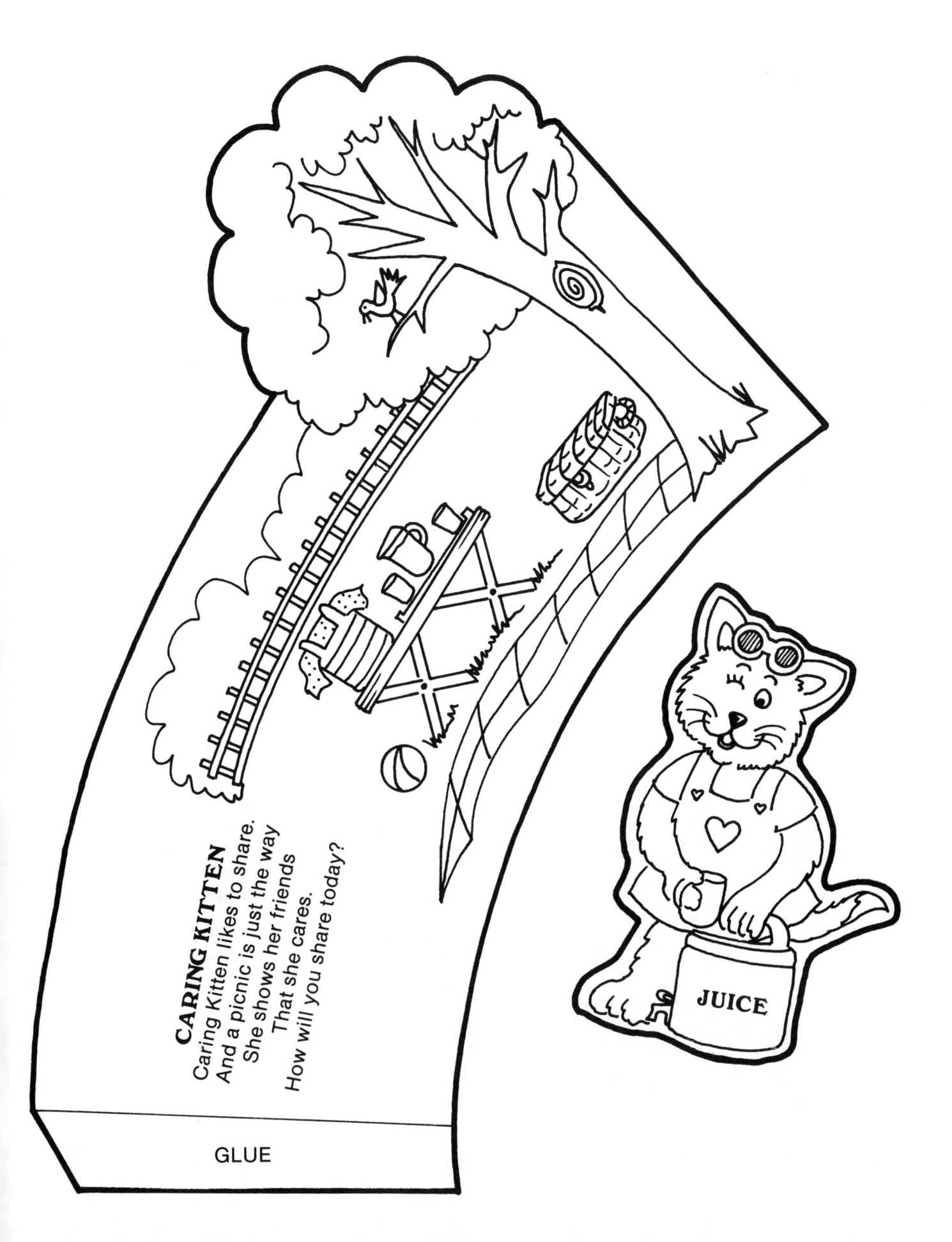

Caring Kitten likes to share.
And a picnic is just the way
She shows her friends
That she cares.
How will you share today?

GLUE

JUICE

GOD'S FAVORITE POEM

All the "self-portraits" for this poem will help children learn that God loves them no matter what mood they're in at the moment. Reproduce the circles on tagboard. The sticks should be cut from cardboard.

MATERIALS:

8 puppet circles
Puppet stick
Crayons
Scissors
Hole punch
Piece of yarn or string

DIRECTIONS:

1. Draw your face in all the circles, showing how you look when you're happy, mad, sad, etc.
2. Cut out circles and punch holes on the dots.
3. Put the circles in order and string together with stick.
4. Hold stick in one hand and flip the faces as you read the poem. Remember God loves you no matter what you're feeling.

GOD'S FAVORITE POEM

God loves me when I'm happy.
God loves me when I'm mad.
God loves me when I'm frightened.
God loves me when I'm sad.

God loves me when I'm smiling.
God loves me when I frown.
God loves me when I'm sleeping
And do not make a sound.

God loves us when we work and play.
God loves us when we rest.
Of all the creatures we can name,
God loves us each the best.

HAPPY

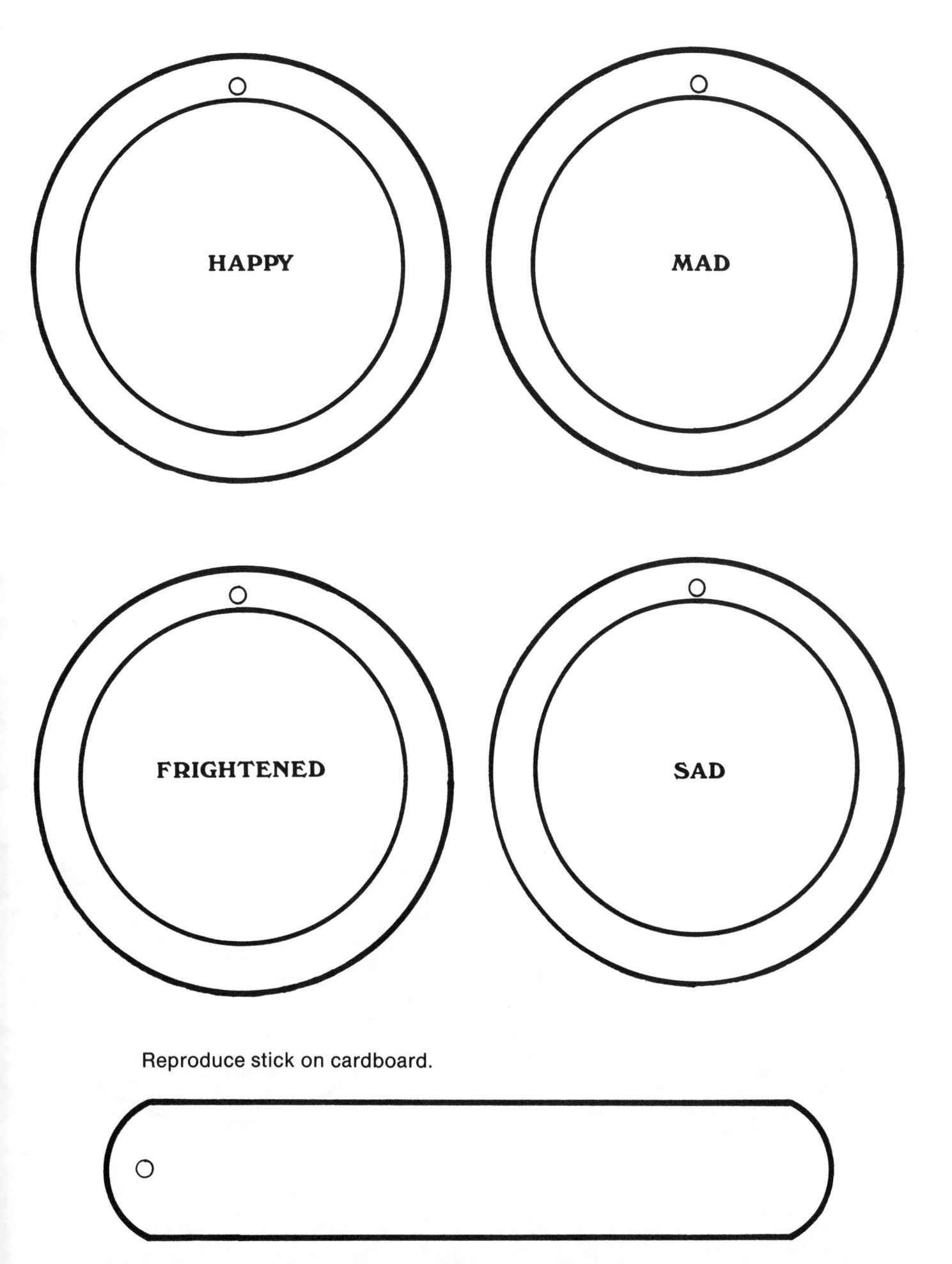

MAD

FRIGHTENED

SAD

Reproduce stick on cardboard.

SMILING

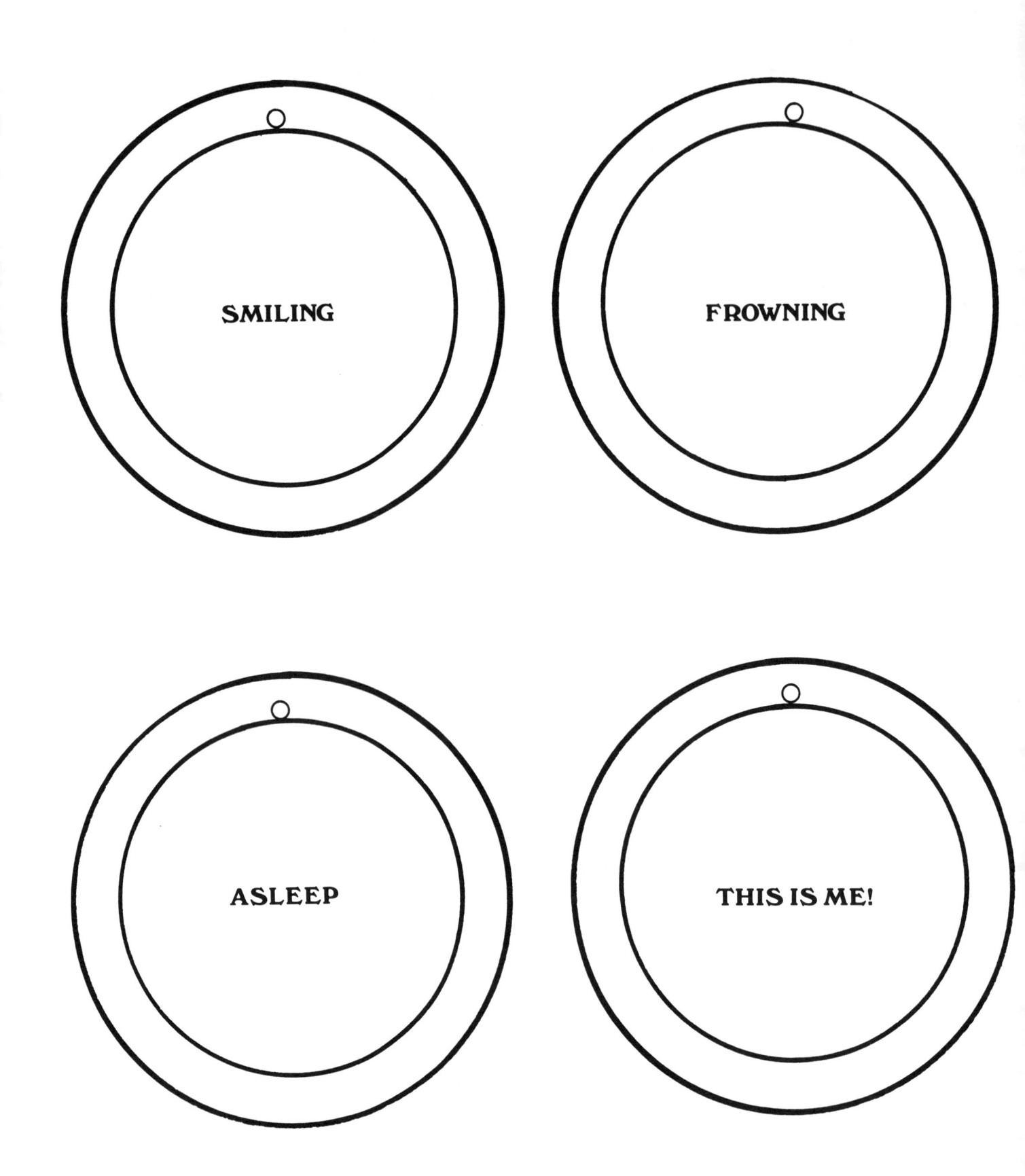

FROWNING

ASLEEP

THIS IS ME!

CLOTH AND CARDBOARD ROLL PUPPET

Here is one puppet that can take on many characters.

MATERIALS:

Cardboard toilet paper rolls
Hand puppet pattern
2 pieces of felt or other fabric
Crayons
Yarn
Scissors
Needle and thread

DIRECTIONS:

1. Cut two hand puppet patterns (see page 94) from fabric.
2. Sew together with needle and thread.
3. Cut cardboard tube in half.
4. Color a face on the tube.
5. Cut yarn in 8" lengths for hair. Tie together in the middle.
6. Glue hair to sides of face.
7. Slip puppet over your hand. Add the head and make your puppet act as you like.
8. Make more heads for your puppet so that you can change characters.

PUPPET PATTERN

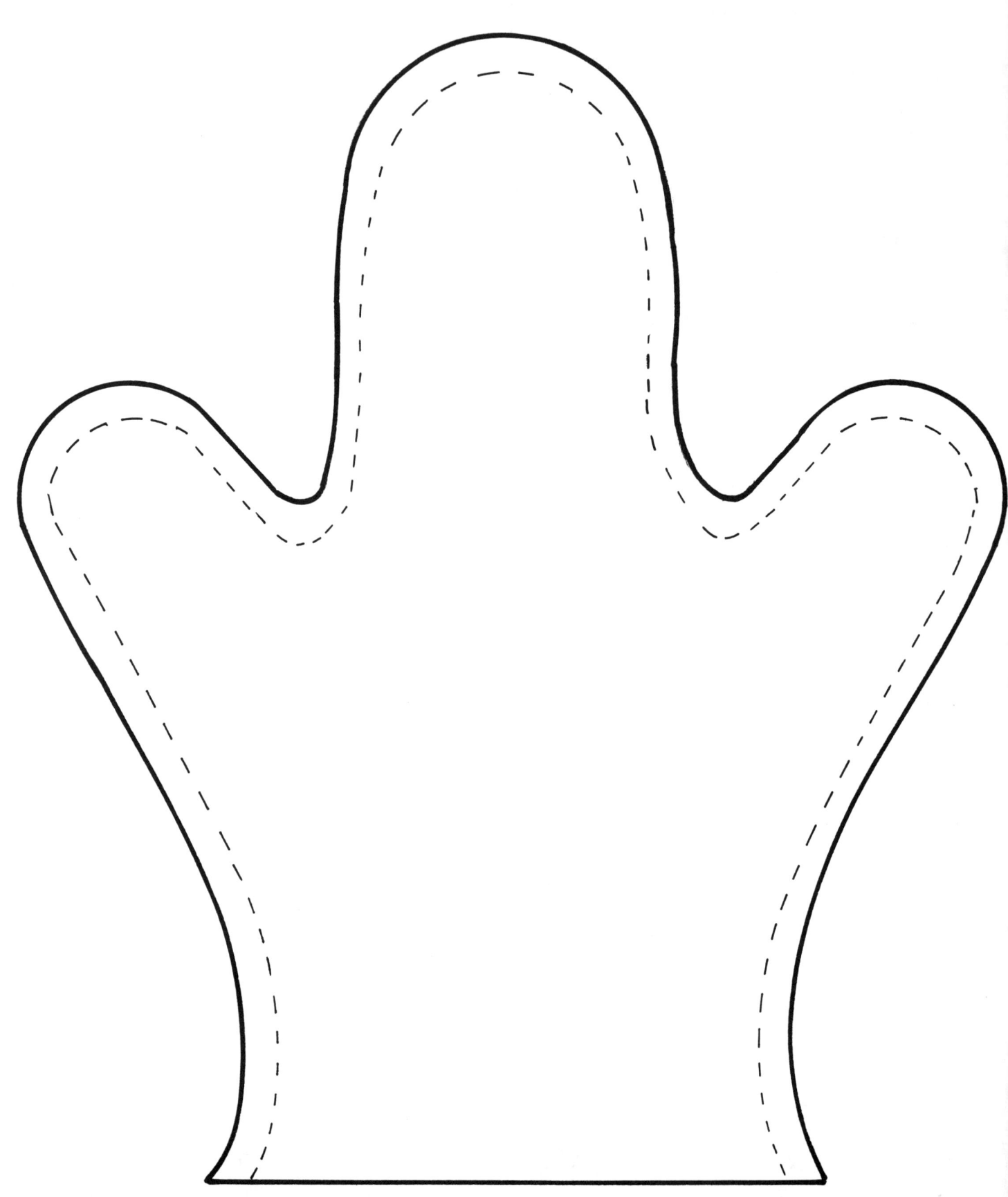

DAISY POEM AND PUPPET

Talk with your students about God's acceptance of us all. Did you know daisies can come in pink, blue, gold and yellow as well as white? Have your students color their daisy puppets their own special way and use them when reciting the poem on a warm summer day. Reproduce both pieces on tagboard.

DAISY POEM

Daisies grow in my garden path.
Some are straight and tall;
Some are short and crooked;
Some hardly grow at all.
But put them all together;
It's a lovely sight to see!
God loves each daisy, tall or short,
As God loves you and me.

DIRECTIONS:

1. Cut out the puppet. Color in your favorite daisy color.
2. Assemble as shown in diagram.
3. Slip fingers through the back of the puppet and move it as you say the poem.

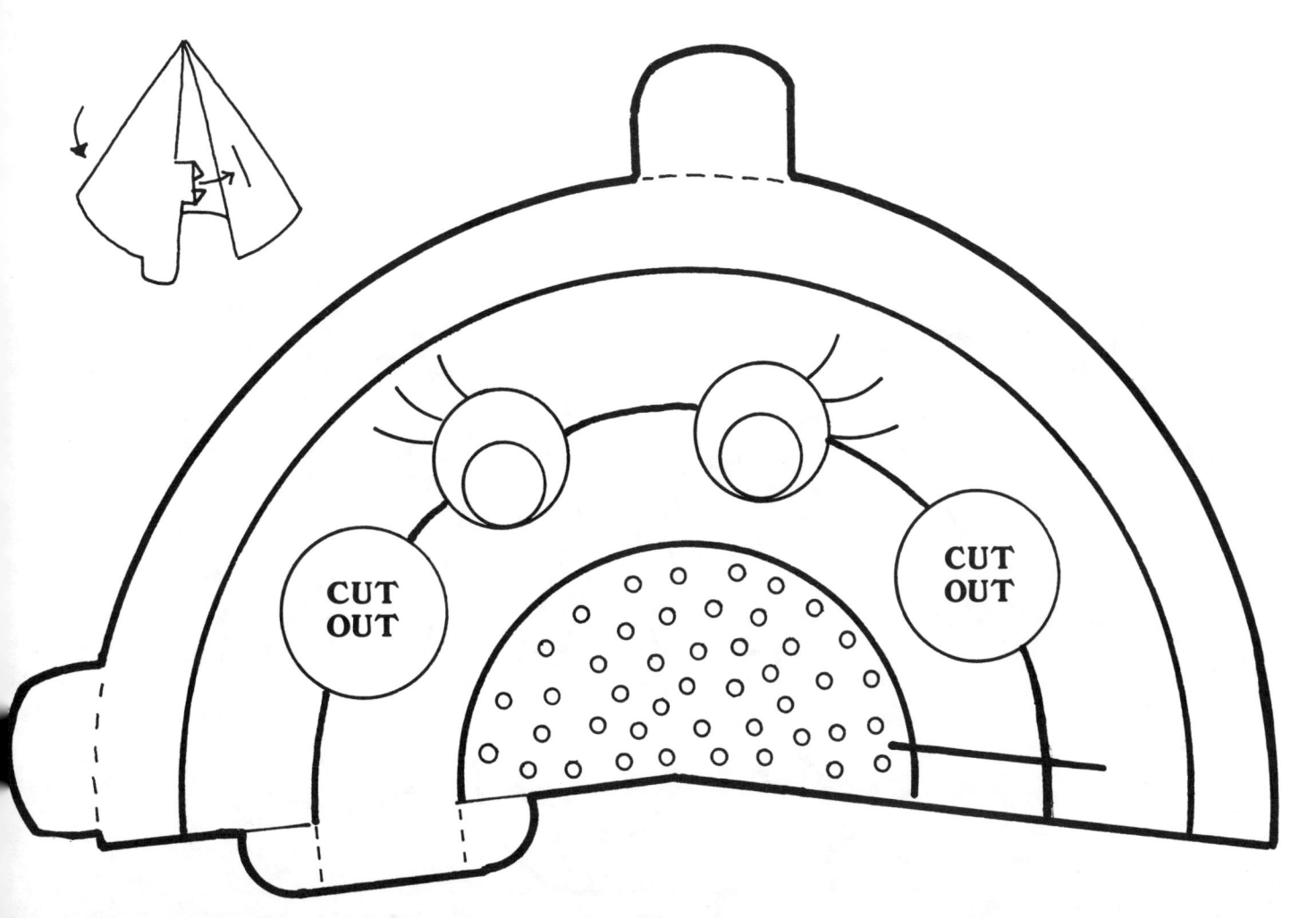

DAISY PATTERN

back